ENDS OF EMPIRE

ENDS OF EMPIRE

Women and Ideology in Early Eighteenth-Century English Literature

Laura Brown

Cornell University Press

Ithaca and London

First published 1993 by Cornell University Press.

International Standard Book Number 0-8014-2850-5 (cloth)
International Standard Book Number 0-8014-8095-7 (paper)
Library of Congress Catalog Card Number 92-36853

Printed in the United States of America

Librarians: Library of Congress cataloging information appears on the last page of the book.

⊗ The paper in this book meets the minimum requirements of the American National Standard for Information Sciences— Permanence of Paper for Printed Library Materials, ANSI Z39.48-1984.

This book is dedicated to my mother and father
Joan Elizabeth Schaefer Brown
Kenneth Francis Brown

Pōmaika'i wale
ke keiki 'ohana

Contents

Acknowledgments

Some of the materials in this book have been previously published. I am grateful to be able to make use of them here. A version of Chapter 1 appeared as "The Romance of Empire: *Oroonoko* and the Trade in Slaves," in *The New Eighteenth Century: Theory, Politics, English Literature*, ed. Felicity Nussbaum and Laura Brown (Methuen: New York, 1987), 41–61. Several pages and some portions of the argument from Chapter 2 appeared as "The Defenseless Woman and the Development of English Tragedy," in *Studies in English Literature* 22 (1982): 429–43. And a version of Chapter 5 appeared as "Reading Race and Gender: Jonathan Swift," in *Eighteenth-Century Studies* 23 (1990): 424–43.

I am also grateful for the assistance and criticism of students, colleagues, and friends. I would like to thank Judith Frank, Jeffrey Nunokawa, Felicity Nussbaum, Mary Jacobus, Shirley Samuels, Mark Seltzer, the graduate students in "Colonialism and Eighteenth-Century Literature" (Cornell, Spring 1988), Sheila Lloyd, Ben Halm, the graduate students in "Literary Anti-Feminism in the Eighteenth Century" (Cornell, Fall 1991), Eleanor Courtemanche, and Jia-ming Han. Walter Cohen's advice and support stand behind every argument, every passage, and especially many substantial footnotes in this book. My best work is to his credit.

At this point in another life I might have thanked my children for allowing me to absent myself from their company on so many occasions during the writing of this book. But in fact they did no such thing, and neither did I. Under such circumstances, I am not sure to what or to whom I owe the completion of the project. But I am sure that I owe the constant renewal of my commitment to the end that this book is designed to serve to Moana I'i Brown-Cohen and Jonah Isaac Brown-Cohen, and to their little brother.

L. B.

Ithaca, New York

ENDS OF EMPIRE

1

The Feminization of Ideology:
An Introduction

> The Seeds of Punning are in the Minds of all Men, and tho'
> they may be subdued by Reason, Reflection and good Sense,
> they will be very apt to shoot up in the greatest Genius, that is
> not broken and cultivated by the Rules of Art. . . . there is no
> Question, but as [punning] has sunk in one Age and rose in
> another, it will again recover it self in some distant Period of
> Time, as Pedantry and Ignorance shall prevail upon Wit and
> Sense. . . . In short, one may say of a Punn as the Country-
> man described his Nightingale, that it is *vox & prætereà nihil*, a
> Sound, and nothing but a Sound.
>
> Joseph Addison, *Spectator* no. 61

The title of this book, "ends" of empire, is a political
pun. It is meant to evoke the ways in which the literature of
the eighteenth century served the purpose of empire, and
also the ways in which a radical critique might recruit that
literature to uncover the operations of imperialism in the
eighteenth century and to help put a stop to empire in the
twentieth. I will return to the politics of these assertions,
and I will even turn, in the discussion of male sexuality in
Chapter 4, to at least one of the other meanings of "ends,"
a less lofty and more corporeal "end" so often epitomized
in this period by "Lord Fanny." But first I must make a
concession to Joseph Addison and to the Augustan attack
on punning as a form of false wit which I have cited in
the epigraph to this chapter. In defining and condemning

1

punning, Addison tells us that the critic's job is "to distinguish the several kinds of Wit by Terms of Art, and to consider them as more or less perfect, according as they were founded in Truth."[1] Though obviously I do not share this Augustan aversion to word play, truth will be my watchword, too, as it was for Addison. The ends of these critical readings are founded on a polemical assertion of truth. And in the last chapter of this book I turn to the question of the truth in Gulliver's claim "to say the truth" about colonialism, and to my own claim to a true radical political criticism.

My truth, like Swift's in his account of Gulliver's ultimate anti-imperialist pronouncements, is less prescriptive and more constructive than it might seem. Like the punning in my title, the truth laid out by this book is decidedly, even systematically, un-Addisonian. It is constructed out of contradiction and disjunction; it takes the form of mutual interaction and articulation; and most important, it defines a common political project. It is not the self-confident, monolithic truth of the Augustans; it differs generically from those famous Popean assertions, "Most Women have no Characters at all" or "WHATEVER IS, IS RIGHT."[2] The truth of this study emerges partly from a demystification of the Augustan truth that Addison evokes in his attack on punning and false wit or Pope presents in his assessment of female nature. But it also comes in part, I willingly concede, from the categories and the ironies of eighteenth-century literary culture itself. My project does not—indeed cannot—dissever itself from its subject: I have learned

1. Joseph Addison, *Spectator* no. 61 (10 May 1711), in *The Spectator*, ed. Donald F. Bond, 5 vols. (Oxford: Clarendon Press, 1965), 1:262.

2. Alexander Pope, *Epistle to a Lady*, line 2, in *Epistles to Several Persons (Moral Essays)*, ed. F. W. Bateson (London: Methuen; New Haven: Yale University Press, 1951); *Essay on Man*, IV.394, ed. Maynard Mack (London: Methuen, 1950).

more from Joseph Addison and Alexander Pope than from any other experts on eighteenth-century literary culture. In particular, the process of demystification that guides my work depends on the very figure to which Addison turns in the sentence immediately succeeding this passage from the essay on punning—the figure that stands as the opposite of the "Punn," that of a "fine Woman." What is the "fine Woman" doing in Addison's abstract account of true and false wit? She appears in the epigraph to Chapter 4, which continues this excerpt from the *Spectator*. In that chapter, I examine in detail the specific connections between this "fine Woman" and "true Wit." But Addison's turn to the female figure, and his general participation in the eighteenth-century preoccupation with the category of gender, gives me a hint about how to read this literature and in fact anticipates the method of my study as a whole.

My project too engages fundamentally with the figure of the woman in early eighteenth-century literary culture. I examine the representation of women in the context of mercantile capitalism and of the various issues arising from that historical conjuncture. The book moves from 1688 (the publication date of *Oroonoko*) to 1730 (the approximate terminus of Swift's production of his "Irish tracts"), thus roughly spanning the time from the Restoration to the fall of Walpole. This is the first major age of English imperialism, the age of the powerful consolidation of a consensus on the universal benefits of economic expansion, and of an energetic, wide-ranging, but incomplete ideological hegemony. The female figure, through its simultaneous connections with commodification and trade on the one hand, and violence and difference on the other, plays a central role in the constitution of this mercantile capitalist ideology. That claim is my governing thesis: the representation of women grounds my argument about the nature of imperialist ideology itself; about the functions of commodification, accu-

mulation, and the images of the slave or the colonized native; and ultimately about the question of resistance to the
dominant ideology.

This introductory chapter defines the assumptions shaping my project, places them in relation to other work in
eighteenth-century English studies, and describes their political implications and my political goals. I then summarize
the subsequent chapters, attending to the methods and
materials with which they are engaged and the common
themes that they develop. Finally, I end this essay by pro-
posing a theoretical paradigm, a model of the ideological
nature of eighteenth-century literature as seen through the
representation of women. This model will serve as a guide
for the ensuing discussion and also as a summary statement
of the critical contribution of the study as a whole.

In this book I take mercantile capitalism and its major
consequences—imperialism and commodification—as a
ground. Through readings of literary materials in various
genres and from various social contexts, I describe how
early eighteenth-century literature functions in relation to
these forces of modern history. My claim for the relevance
of mercantile capitalism to this literature is based on the
conviction that literature is significantly implicated with history, and on the specific notion that capitalism and imperialism had a powerful priority in early eighteenth-century
England.

In the focal period of this book, we find the development
of capitalist England's first major overseas empire, the primary phase of the economic exploitation of slaves, and the
substantial growth of a consumer economy. This era is
marked at its outset by the successful trade wars with the
Dutch in the decade following the Restoration, the negotiated resolution in the 1680s of the succession crisis in favor
of Parliament, and the completion of the bourgeois revolu-

tion. It ends with the fall of Walpole, the proliferating political problems in the American colonies, increased imperial rivalry with the French, a growing cultural ambivalence
and nostalgia, and the shift from an obsession with commodification to an interest in the antiquarian, the Gothic,
and the sublime. At home, the early eighteenth-century
witnessed the growth of a money economy; the establishment of the Bank of England and a permanent national
debt; the rise of public credit, investment, stock specula-
tion, and insurance; the extension of urban centers; and
the depopulation of the countryside. Abroad, the Peace of
Utrecht in 1713 signaled England's emergence as a major
imperial power. European overseas expansion began in the
Renaissance, with the Spanish, Portuguese, and Dutch taking the lead. But England, having defeated Holland in the
1660s, surpassed Spain in the early eighteenth century, and
by the 1760s France as well. The bureaucratized and bourgeois profile of this new English empire set the model for
future imperialist ventures by favoring economic motives
over territorial, a shift in emphasis that may have shaped
the modern world more decisively than any other historical
force.

Critiques of empire are neither new nor unique to literary criticism; anti-imperialist writing in Europe begins in
the early sixteenth century. But a concern with the relevance of empire to literary study, with few exceptions, has
only emerged in the mid 1980s. Indeed, this extended si-
lence suggests an implicit ratification of imperialism in aca-
demic criticism in English—a complicity by neglect on the
part of the very cultural tradition in which such a neglect is
least justifiable, but perhaps most likely. England and the
West have been the beneficiaries of empire; their prosperity and cultural vitality are partly products of their global
power. Students of English and Western European culture
would seem to have a special obligation to examine this

prosperity. But a critique of empire, even one directed at past literature, raises fundamental questions about the role of Western Europe and the United States in world history. Furthermore, in eighteenth-century studies the implicit ratification of imperialism has been exacerbated by the traditional conservatism of the field. Until very recently, literary criticism of the period has stressed stability and humanism, the cultural authority of the man of letters, the establishment of the canon, the codification of the language, and the institutionalization of literary criticism itself.

I have tried elsewhere to trace the trajectory of eighteenth-century English studies as it has been formulated in America from the mid-twentieth century on, and to account for its resistance to recent theoretically and politically informed approaches.[3] In brief, the major critics who defined the field—R. S. Crane, William Wimsatt, Earl Wasserman, and Reuben Brower—were all, despite their corollary interests in intellectual history, essentially formalists.[4] Their work thus could not challenge the interpretation of the period shaped by the Whig historians of the nineteenth century, an interpretation that emphasized long-term political stability and cultural coherence. Even the interdisciplinary project of the American Society for Eighteenth-Century Studies—formed in part as a corrective to the hegemony of the New Criticism—did not produce an historical reevaluation of the period, since its notion of "interdisciplinary" was based on the empiricist political and intellectual history

3. Laura Brown, "Revising Critical Practices: An Introductory Essay," in *The New Eighteenth Century: Theory, Politics, English Literature*, ed. Felicity Nussbaum and Laura Brown (New York: Methuen, 1987), 1–22.

4. R. S. Crane, *Critics and Criticism: Essays in Method* (Chicago: University of Chicago Press, 1957); William K. Wimsatt and Cleanth Brooks, *Literary Criticism: A Short History* (New York: Knopf, 1957); Earl Wasserman, *The Subtler Language: Critical Readings of Neoclassic and Romantic Poems* (Baltimore: Johns Hopkins University Press, 1958); Reuben Brower, *Alexander Pope: The Poetry of Allusion* (London: Oxford University Press, 1968).

dominant in the United States until recently. This neglect of the historical materials that indicate cultural crisis—intercultural collision, institutionalized racism, class tension, and changes in women's roles in the family and economy—was matched by a conceptual resistance to political criticism and to "theory," whether defined as poststructuralism, Marxism, Foucauldianism, feminism, or the broad area designated by the interrelated topics of race, ethnicity, minority discourse, and post colonialism. Thus situated, critics of eighteenth-century literature have come to the categories of empire, slavery, and colonialism even later than have Anglo-American literary studies in general.

This conservative profile of eighteenth-century English studies began to shift in the early 1980s. Poststructuralist work in predominantly appreciative formalist accounts—notably William Dowling's book on Boswell, William Warner's and Terry Castle's on Richardson, and G. Douglas Atkins's on Dryden and Pope[5]—was the first visible intervention. As the interest in Richardson suggests, the novel initially provided the most fertile field for new approaches. Indeed, novel studies have represented something of a deviation from this conservative paradigm. Here, sociological, historical, and even economic accounts played a prominent role, even as other prose forms, poetry, and satire were being read in terms of neoclassicism, Augustan humanism, formal complexity, or aesthetic value. Ian Watt's *Rise of the Novel* (1957) was a powerful progenitor for work on this genre in the United States. Its publication was followed by

5. William Dowling, *Language and Logos in Boswell's "Life of Johnson"* (Princeton: Princeton University Press, 1981); G. Douglas Atkins, *Reading Deconstruction, Deconstructive Readings* (Lexington: University of Kentucky Press, 1983); William Warner, *Reading Clarissa: The Struggles of Interpretation* (New Haven: Yale University Press, 1979); Terry Castle, *Clarissa's Ciphers: Meaning and Disruption in Richardson's "Clarissa"* (Ithaca: Cornell University Press, 1982).

8   Ends of Empire

prominent studies by Maximillian Novak and John Richetti in the 1960s, and theirs by the contributions of Terry Eagleton, Lennard Davis, and Michael McKeon in the 1980s.[6]

This new work belongs both to the venerable leftist sociological tradition of Watt and to an emergent and more widespread movement in the criticism of other literary forms in the period. Since the mid-1980s, for the first time in modern eighteenth-century studies, approaches to other genres have become methodologically congruent with approaches to the novel. In this recent period, views of eighteenth-century English literature—including the novel—have taken a variety of forms, including Marxist, new historicist or Foucauldian, and feminist. A diverse collection of studies has offered fresh perspectives on writers such as Pope, Swift, and Fielding and topics such as domestic ideology, social control, popular literature, women's poetry, and autobiography.[7] These studies themselves respond to a major shift in Anglo-American historiography, which has

6. Ian Watt, *The Rise of the Novel: Studies in Defoe, Richardson and Fielding* (London: Chatto and Windus, 1957); Maximillian E. Novak, *Economics and the Fiction of Daniel Defoe* (Berkeley and Los Angeles: University of California Press, 1962); John J. Richetti, *Popular Fiction before Richardson: Narrative Patterns, 1700–1739* (Oxford: Clarendon Press, 1969); Terry Eagleton, *The Rape of Clarissa: Writing, Sexuality and Class Struggle in Samuel Richardson* (Oxford: Basil Blackwell, 1982); Lennard Davis, *Factual Fictions: The Origins of the English Novel* (New York: Columbia University Press, 1983); Michael McKeon, *The Origins of the English Novel, 1660–1740* (Baltimore: Johns Hopkins University Press, 1987). Though Watt and Eagleton belong in significant ways to the British tradition, their books have been sufficiently influential in the United States to merit inclusion here.

7. Carole Fabricant, *Swift's Landscape* (Baltimore: Johns Hopkins University Press, 1982); Ellen Pollak, *The Poetics of Sexual Myth: Gender and Ideology in the Verse of Swift and Pope* (Chicago: University of Chicago Press, 1985); Nancy Armstrong, *Desire and Domestic Fiction: A Political History of the Novel* (New York: Oxford University Press, 1987); John B. Bender, *Imagining the Penitentiary: Fiction and the Architecture of Mind in Eighteenth-Century England* (Chicago: University of Chicago Press, 1987); Carol Kay, *Political Constructions: Defoe, Richardson, and Sterne in Relation to Hobbes, Hume, and Burke* (Ithaca: Cornell University Press, 1988); Felicity Nussbaum, *The Autobiographical Subject: Gender and Ideology in Eigh-*

gradually come to raise issues of popular and working-class
culture, consumerism, criminality, colonialism and cultural
difference, social control and surveillance, marriage and
the family, and sexuality and gender definition, among
others.[8]

The questions posed by this new work are implicitly an-
tithetical to the concerns with political stability, cultural
consolidation, canonical authority, and formal complexity
or elegance that previously dominated the views of the period. There has not, however, been a paradigm shift in this
field, as there has in Renaissance studies or Romanticism.
Traditional work often continues to represent the eighteenth century in its self-definition as well as its public pro-
fessional image. My project thus situates itself in relation

teenth-Century England (Baltimore: Johns Hopkins University Press, 1989);
Dianne Dugaw, *Warrior Women and Popular Balladry, 1650–1850* (Cambridge: Cambridge University Press, 1989); Donna Landry, *The Muses of
Resistance: Laboring-Class Women's Poetry in Britain, 1739–1796* (Cambridge:
Cambridge University Press, 1990); Jill Campbell, *Natural Masques: Gender
and Identity in Fielding's Plays and Novels* (Stanford: Stanford University
Press, 1993). My work, of course, builds upon and diverges from all of
these earlier studies. In particular, despite a superficial resemblance of
orientation, Nancy Armstrong's claims for women's access to domestic
power are actually incompatible with the argument advanced here, as is
her grounding notion of the essential role of discursive forms, and particularly the novel, in the production of major bourgeois social structures.
And Carol Kay's notion of "political" construction, again despite a political
terminology similar to mine, refers to the context of contemporary political formulation rather than to the constitution of ideology.

8. Some examples might include E. P. Thompson, *Whigs and Hunters:
The Origin of the Black Act* (New York: Pantheon, 1975); Natalie Zemon
Davis, *Society and Culture in Early Modern France: Eight Essays* (Stanford:
Stanford University Press, 1975); Lawrence Stone, *The Family, Sex and
Marriage in England, 1500–1800* (New York: Harper and Row, 1977); Neil
McKendrick, John Brewer, and J. H. Plumb, *The Birth of a Consumer Soci-
ety: The Commercialization of Eighteenth-Century England* (Bloomington: Indi-
ana University Press, 1982); Sidney Wilfred Mintz, *Sweetness and Power:
The Place of Sugar in Modern History* (New York: Viking, 1985); Bridget
Hill, *Women, Work, and Sexual Politics in Eighteenth-Century England* (Oxford: Basil Blackwell, 1989); Susan Staves, *Married Women's Separate Property in England, 1660–1833* (Cambridge: Harvard University Press, 1990).

both to eighteenth-century studies as traditionally defined
and to the most recent revisionist work in the period.

In response to those traditional perspectives on eighteenth-century studies, I have designed the chapters that
follow to change the dominant self-definition and public
image of the field, and I have tried to pose this specifically
revisionist undertaking as starkly as possible. Traditional
critics have implied that this period cannot be understood
without an appreciative reverence for the man of letters, a
predominantly sympathetic reading of individual texts, and
an attention to the contexts of neoclassicism, Augustanism,
and humanism. To counter these assumptions, I place
eighteenth-century literature in the context of mercantile
capitalism, a category that I argue cannot be understood
without an analysis of the representation of women. Such
an assertion may be ambitious, but by making it I am not
dismissing prior work or prior, equally ambitious, assumptions. Rather, I am matching one powerful set of presup-
positions with another. My purpose is to bring the category
of imperialism up to the developmental level of a group of
widely accepted perspectives from which gender and empire are largely excluded, and thus to stake out a new ter-
rain for investigation.

But of course this book also belongs to that loosely defined critical movement in which issues of race, gender,
class, sexuality, and cultural difference have displaced
those of political stability and aesthetic value. In this context, my enterprise does not seem so ambitious or original
in its materials and methods, and my claim for the relevance of gender and empire is much less distinctive. Here,
however, my end is political rather than methodological: to
provide an explicit agenda for the recent changes in the
field of eighteenth-century literary studies. I do not mean
to exclude other views of the significance of this new work,
but rather to bring those views to consciousness by presenting one self-consciously politicized position.

Specifically, then, I want to reorient the project of eighteenth-century literary studies toward an integrated account of categories of oppression so that the examination of this field can promote the ends of a feminist, anti-imperialist, anti-racist, libertarian politics. Many readers may object to these methods and aims. I welcome objections, in the belief that disagreements on matters of principle—methodological, theoretical, and political—can be productive. In that spirit, I have structured my presentation to make clear the bases for agreement or disagreement in order to stimulate debate and promote positive revision

My political ends are linked to my propositions about eighteenth-century literary culture. By insisting upon the relevance of mercantile capitalism, I have positioned myself to engage with a dominant ideology, especially as it relates to issues of oppression. Thus situated, in this study I extract from that founding engagement a series of political models. First, the structural relationships among a hegemonic ideology and positions of resistance invite a critical method concerned with articulation. Thus, throughout these readings, I seek out dialectical relationships among positions of oppression. I connect categories of difference primarily to one another, rather than exclusively to the dominant ideology, and in so doing I accord a degree of autonomy even to those positions that seem most effectively incorporated by structures of power.

This emphasis on the potential for opposition has implications for critiques of imperialism or of ideology in general. Ideology critique becomes a means of recovering past progressive positions, and also a basis for supporting radical change in our own period by making the literature of those in power politically usable to those in opposition. How can this book be used for such an end? Feminists might find insights into the multiple forces that maintain female subordination today in these descriptions of the complex role of the female figure in the eighteenth century. Activists working for cultural diversity might be able to find modern connections among seemingly disparate positions through analogies to the mutually dependent situations of women, slaves, blacks, colonizers, and colonized defined in these readings. More generally, a radical intelligentsia might be able to use an account of imperialist ideology in this period to analyze modern crises, or to delegitimize some of the dominant institutions of modern society.

The enterprise of recovering positions of resistance also addresses the nature of ideology itself; attending to resistance in effect defines ideology as potentially fissured rather than monolithic. In emphasizing these fissures, I hope to contribute to the current debate about the political purpose of recent political criticism. New historicist work in particular, in its engagement with the discursive functionings of power, has been attacked for privileging systems of oppression at the expense of marginal perspectives. That attack has been answered in more recent studies, often deeply influenced by new historicism, that focus on issues of gender, race, sexuality, and even class. I have already mentioned my aim to politicize the recent interest in contestatory materials within eighteenth-century studies. In the broader context of Anglo-American criticism, my work here has a similar purpose: to contribute to the recent move to remedy the deficiencies of a political criticism oriented toward power by calling attention to marginal positions, and to extend that pragmatic enterprise in the direction of self-conscious politicization and explicit theorization.

A brief survey of the chapters that follow illustrates my political claims. Each of these readings brings together apparently incongruous categories in order to reveal the nature of a dominant ideological structure and to suggest its implicit dissonances. In arranging these readings, I have sought to weave together various perspectives on the function of the female figure in relation to mercantile capitalist thought and to generate from this interweaving a theory of the role of the representation of women in early eighteenth-century literature.

In Chapter 2 I begin the process with an account of a prominent narrative on the topic of slavery written by a woman. In Aphra Behn's *Oroonoko* the figure of the woman—both the narrator and her proxies in the action—serves as a mediator through which the forces of mercantile capitalism are represented in the language of heroic romance. The woman is an object both of romantic admiration and of commodification. She inspires the hero's chivalric exercises; she also gains through trade the trinkets that epitomize colonialist exploitation and the dress that embodies the feminization of imperialist accumulation. Her ambiguous position enables the narrative to use the romanticized image of the African slave Oroonoko to represent the historical crisis of slavery. That is, the female figure provides the novella with an access to history, so that the slave can be seen, finally, as an historical presence in his own right and his own body. Oroonoko is Europeanized and naturalized, but he also powerfully evokes the brutal realities of the Caribbean slave trade. Thus the woman and the slave are significantly connected in this narrative, even though their positions and roles differ substantially. An account of their relationship makes it possible to see how Behn's novella draws upon the conventions of heroic romance and at the same time engages vividly with the fate of a racially, geographically distant figure, how this text is bound to an imperialist perspective while at the same time transcending that perspective.

In Chapter 6, I make a parallel effort to link race and gender by moving from Swift's misogynist poetry, to his Irish tracts, and then to *Gulliver's Travels*. This series of conjunctions is complicated by the self-effacing structure of commodification as it functions in Swift's works, by its elusive movement into sexuality and its related conflation with the female body. Swift's poetry attacks women for an essential corruption, but the Irish tracts join the attack on the nauseous female body by criticizing female luxury, accumulation, and consumption. From this perspective, Gulliver's various connections with women in Lilliput and Brobdingnag are attempts to establish an identity in the face of a pervasive commodification. The fourth voyage takes the text into the realm of contemporary accounts of race, specifically descriptions of the Negro in Africa. The Yahoo is Swift's prototypical woman—a figure of essential corruption like that in the misogynist poetry—and also an extended imitation of contemporary descriptions of the African native. In the Yahoo, then, the female other and the native other are superimposed, and Gulliver's contradictory movement between aversion to and incorporation by both figures exposes the crisis of colonialist identity, the reciprocal, problematic relationship between colonizer and colonized.

Chapters 2 and 6 frame the book. At opposite historical ends of my enterprise, they provide the most complex examples of the integrative approach I seek to define here: in different ways they join issues of gender and race. Both found this conjunction upon the problem of commodification, the association of the female figure with accumulation, consumption, and the products of trade. As we will see, commodification is one of the most frequent means by which imperialist ideology utilizes the figure of the woman. Indeed, the literary engagement with commodification— both positive and negative—prominently contributes to the feminization of mercantile capitalist thought, in which apologies for empire and attacks on its domestic implications are expressed through the female figure.

Chapters 3 and 4—my essays on the she-tragedy and on aesthetic writing—are centrally concerned with this feminization of the dominant ideology. Thomas Otway's *The Orphan* and Nicholas Rowe's *Jane Shore*, the main texts of Chapter 3, illustrate how an economically overdetermined definition of female sexuality—variously represented as passivity and victimization—is ideologically reinscribed as commodification. The protagonists of these plays are distinctively weak, suffering, and helpless; they embody a culturally significant devaluation of the female figure generated in part by the contemporary economic devaluation of women's labor that resulted from the demise of domestic production and the increasing prominence of a consumer economy. Their constitutive passivity forms the basis for the she-tragedy's definition of female sexuality as suffering. For Jane Shore, that suffering sexuality is transposed in the final, most affecting scenes of the play into commodification. The commodified woman, like the passive, helpless one, derives from the contemporary conjuncture of capitalism and consumption through a process that depends upon a female sexuality constituted by violence and rape.

Sexuality is thus another persistent problem connected with the feminization of mercantile capitalist ideology. In Swift's works, as we have seen, detailed images of the sexualized female body arise through his critique of female commodification. That body, both sexually attractive and repellent, becomes the figurative basis for Gulliver's crisis of identity and thus for the problematization of colonialist ideology. In Chapter 4 I bring sexuality and commodification together again in a discussion of aesthetic theory. Here, the metaphorical feminization of early eighteenth-century aesthetic writing—in which true wit is commonly a woman—parallels the feminization of mercantile capitalist ideology, and ties aesthetics to empire. The debate about the nature of true wit thus expresses the problematic ideo-

logical consequences of commodification. In both cases
the true nature of the woman is the defining paradox—
whether dress compromises female beauty or constitutes it,
and whether the surface of female adornment can be pene-
trated to reveal a discernible and stable character. The
elaboration of this paradox extends through commodification to sexuality: the female figure beneath the dress is often unambiguously a sexual object. In Pope's poetry that
female sexual object becomes quite suddenly and unexpectedly a male figure in a moment of sexual humiliation.
Here the undressed woman serves as a proxy for a crisis of
male sexuality, a crisis seemingly brought about through
female commodification. This last erotic turn on commodification and true wit reveals a process typical in the
feminization of mercantile capitalist ideology: women become the proxies for men, object and agent of accumulation are reversed, and thus the female figure is made to
bear responsibility for empire.

In Chapter 5, "Amazons and Africans," I open with that
notion of the scapegoating of women. The Amazon of Restoration and eighteenth-century literary and popular culture is a versatile, usually misogynist trope that typically
works to deny the consequences of empire. The version of
the Amazon in Dryden's imitation of Juvenal's sixth satire
serves as a model for the uses of the trope in eighteenth-
century imperialist ideology. Dryden's Amazons assume the
role of men by dressing in military garb and fighting as
gladiators. They are cruel, murderous figures of social dis-
integration, whose prevalence is attributed to imperial dec-
adence. Their domestic violence displaces male imperialist
violence, and thereby deflects attention from imperial
power. The protagonist of Defoe's *Roxana* is another ultimately murderous Amazon. Ironically, the scapegoating
role performed by the Amazon image in this text turns
Roxana into an agent in her own right. Roxana is a com-

modified figure, but she comes to control the process of accumulation by becoming a "she-merchant," a "man-woman," an Amazon of mercantile capitalism. The power she acquires in her transition from proxy to agent enables her to voice a radical, protofeminist advocacy of female liberty that is repudiated, however, in her final decline. Thus the Amazon can act both as a proxy and as a figure of radical heterogeneity. In that latter guise, Roxana resembles the representation of the Africans in *Captain Singleton*; both women and natives are defined by their relation to trade, and the native other, like the female other, can shift from object to agent. In fact, the Amazon trope brings the woman and the native to yet another point of rapprochement: the Amazon also stands for racial difference. From classical times through the seventeenth century Amazons were purportedly sighted just beyond the boundaries of the geographically known world. I juxtapose *Captain Singleton* and *Roxana* to show how the threatening ambiguity of the native and the woman place them in a similar relation to a dominant, imperialist ideology.

Thus I move from an account of gender and race under colonialism to the consolidation of a feminist definition of commodification and sexuality, and back again to gender, race, and empire. Such a process reflects my sense of the complexity of these cultural structures and the multiply determined nature of their interactions. I center each chapter around a canonical text or author, not to enhance the appreciative reception of these texts, but to examine their function in the contemporary crises of cultural difference and economic expansion. And though these chapters might be loosely described as "readings" and might—as in the case of *Oroonoko*—provide rather full accounts of single texts, my purpose here is not to explicate but to "read"—in and through the texts—a series of significant and significantly interrelated issues in eighteenth-century literary culture. In the concluding section of this opening chapter, I would like to try to bring some of these issues together, and by that means to propose a working paradigm for the study as a whole.

I take as my ground in this book the historical contingency of English mercantile capitalism, and as my focus the representation of women within that context. Against that ground, I place a series of categories and ideological figures into various relationships with one another and with the historical forces upon which they are constructed. I am more interested in the complexity of the relations among the categories and figures I define here than in their common historical basis in mercantile capitalism. Rather than reduce these interconnections to a simple system of determinants, I want to explore the model of multiple articulations. That effort is the primary methodological import of each of the chapters that follow. Taken together, these chapters comprise a theory of eighteenth-century literature more extensive and I think more powerful than the sum of their individual efforts.

If the figure of the woman occupies a crucial place in the constitution of mercantile capitalist ideology, then one way to define that ideology is to find a pattern in the various interconnected functions of the female figure. That is, grouping and distinguishing the different roles of women in this literature can generate a poetics of imperialist ideology. The figure of the woman seems to present two different faces in the literary culture examined here. First, through an association with trade, commodification, and consumption generated by the economic devaluation of women's labor, woman takes a central position in the representation of such fundamental dimensions of cultural experience as character, identity, and value. The female figure is associated with the mystifying process of fetishization, and with the related problems of identity and knowledge, artifice and reality, dissembling and truth, where the effort of seeing past the objects of accumulation becomes a kind of cultural obsession. In this role the woman typically acts as a proxy for male acquisition or a scapegoat of male violence. The corruption assigned to the female body and the murderousness attributed to the militarized female figure can be understood as a reversal of agent and object characteristic of the process by which capitalist alienation or imperialist violence is occluded. But this persistent scapegoating also opens up the potential for resistance, since it entails the representation of an active female agency. Such an image may provide a locus for protofeminist sentiment—for a radical reading of bourgeois liberty or for an echo of the libertarian notions of the prior, revolutionary period. Whatever its ultimate effect, however, the female figure has a crucial function in this literature, and its consistent efficacy suggests that mercantile capitalist ideology at this point in its development in England is formulated around gender division.

The second major function of the figure of the woman arises from the connection between gender and difference—the radical heterogeneity of sexual, racial, or class dissimilarities. Indeed, though I have moved from commodification to difference, this latter role may more effectively explain the feminization of mercantile capitalist ideology. Perhaps the general utility of the female figure in this ideological complex is due to the powerful association of women with difference, an association that might arise partly from the historically specific process of fetishization itself, but also from transhistorical dimensions of gender division. This second function is represented in terms of the female body and of sexuality, both male and female. As figures of difference, women are connected with sexual insatiability, class instability, natives, the colonized, and the potentially threatening, unassimilable other.

Thus this literature is characterized by a series of articulations in which these two functions—fetishization and difference—confront each other, and various dimensions of each role come into focus or fertile interaction. For instance, the body as image of sexual difference merges with the body as mystified essence beneath the commodified surface of dress. This conflation explains how problems of sexuality seem to arise from issues of dress and adornment; how a disgust with essential corruption can be linked at once to sexual promiscuity and to fetishization; and how concerns with identity can be integrated with ambiguities in sexuality, male or female. Similarly, the female as figure of passivity, which is connected to the devaluation of women's labor and the growth of female consumption, converges with the representation of sexual difference constituted through violence against women and then emerges as commodification. Relatedly, but in the opposite direction, the commodified female figure becomes a powerfully sexualized figure of difference that then serves as the locus for problems of male as well as female sexuality. Likewise, the violence and the instability of identity connected with colonialism combine with the problem of female identity connected with commodification; and relations of commodification under slavery coalesce with figures of female accumulation and consumption.

The result is something more than juxtaposition; these convergences under the general rubrics of fetishization and difference can illuminate a particular issue—identity, sexuality, or misogyny. Or they can unsettle the categories of fetishization and difference themselves, so that, for instance, the interaction of the woman and the slave, as figures of commodification, indicates their common interests and thus transcends difference, however conditionally. Or the transformation from object to agent of commodification suggests how the mystery of the commodity might be solved. And, maybe most interesting politically, the oppositional possibilities raised by the process of proxying under the aegis of commodification matches up with the potential for resistance implied in using female difference as a link to more threatening categories of difference, such as the slave or the native. Through commodification or through difference—women can disturb the coherence of mercantile capitalist ideology either way they come to it, in part because they are so essential to its self-representation.

These conjunctures anticipate larger ones in the practice of criticism and critical theory in general. They provide a concrete staging of the ways in which apparently divergent critical perspectives might be integrated. In doing so they set up a model for the integration of different political interests and thus help to define various forms of critical and political articulation among radical projects. On the basis of these mutual interactions, this study attempts to project a series of potential conjunctions among various schools and orientations: among critics defining themselves as materialist, feminist, or marxist, and those engaged with issues of race, colonialism and postcolonialism, and sexuality. Each of these chapters singly and this book as a whole point to a proposal for a political practice based upon the articulation of different critical perspectives and various political constituencies.

Thus I have designed these readings of some of the ways in which early eighteenth-century literary texts both serve the "ends" of empire and also work to bring about its end in their own period to support a politics that contributes to the end of imperialism in the present day. This modern end is the polemical truth the book claims to serve. It is both a political commitment and a critical method, both an end and a means. It is also both a faith and a conditional construction. I try to show in the course of this study how this truth escapes simple formulation; how it leans upon the cultural structures that it aims to demystify; how it resides in contradiction, irony, and reversal; and how it emerges from the process of articulation itself.

The two ends of empire that I address here sometimes elude easy distinction. I cannot confidently claim, in the end, to be able to separate a text that serves the purposes of empire from the effort to put a stop to it, in the past or the present. A cultural proposition that seems to shore up the status quo and to serve a dominant ideology can sometimes become a perverse means to its undermining—just as Jonathan Swift's canonical misogyny opens up a critique of racism and colonialism. An evident sympathy for those oppressed by imperialism can be profoundly implicated in the dominant ideology from which the forces of empire emanate—just as Behn's attack on slavery is expressed in the language of heroic romance. There is a lesson here. By the same token, a vigorous reading against the grain of literary appreciation and traditional canonicity—such as this one— might likewise escape a single, stable import. A claim to truth that seeks an easy demarcation between one political "end" of empire and another, or that claims to limit the many possible readings of "ends" to a simple political dichotomy, may thus be left, as Addison says, with "a sound, and nothing but a Sound." So I stoop to punning in my title for a reason, and the epigraph from Addison at the opening of this study is a cautionary one. Less cautiously, I shall attempt to rise to travesty in my conclusion.

2

The Romance of Empire:
Oroonoko and
the Trade in Slaves

> Our victims know us by their scars and by their chains, and it
> is this that makes their evidence irrefutable. It is enough that
> they show us what we have made of them for us to realize
> what we have made of ourselves.
> Jean-Paul Sartre, Preface to Frantz Fanon's *The Wretched of the*
> *Earth*

Aphra Behn's novella *Oroonoko; or, The Royal Slave*,
written and published in the summer of the year of the
1688 Revolution in England,[1] no longer needs an extensive
introduction for students of Restoration and eighteenth-
century literature, or even for many critics in other fields.
Oroonoko has almost entered the canon, as works by Behn
and other women writers have been rediscovered and reprinted in the major revisionist projects of recent Anglo-
American feminist criticism. The novella *Oroonoko* and the
dramatic satire *The Rover*, Behn's two most important
works, both saw new printings in the late 1960s and early

1. For the date of composition, see George Guffey, "Aphra Behn's
Oroonoko: Occasion and Accomplishment," in *Two English Novelists: Aphra
Behn and Anthony Trollope*, by George Guffey and Andrew Wright (Los
Angeles: William Andrews Clark Memorial Library, University of Califor-
nia, 1975), 15–16.

1970s,[2] and Behn herself has been the subject of two critical biographies, Maureen Duffy's *Passionate Shepherdess* (1977) and Angeline Goreau's *Reconstructing Aphra* (1980)—the first significant studies since George Woodcock's *Incomparable Aphra* in 1948.[3] But Woodcock was clearly an anomaly: an anarchist critic in the early stages of the Cold War, exploring issues of feminism and racism while others in the field were consolidating the New Critical paradigm. The only prior topic of consequence regarding Behn arose in a brief skirmish initiated by Ernest Bernbaum in 1913 over the historical question of Behn's trip to Guiana, the setting of *Oroonoko*.[4]

Now one can even find *Oroonoko* in the undergraduate curriculum on occasion; according to the *MLA Bibliography* we can read two or three articles on Aphra Behn each year; and the profession boasts an annual conference on Behn

2. Aphra Behn, *The Rover*, ed. Frederick M. Link (Lincoln: University of Nebraska Press, 1967); *Oroonoko; or, The Royal Slave*, intro. by Lore Metzger (New York: Norton, 1973). Subsequent references to *Oroonoko* will be to this edition.

3. Maureen Duffy, *The Passionate Shepherdess: Aphra Behn, 1640–89* (London: Cap, 1977); Angeline Goreau, *Reconstructing Aphra: A Social Biography of Aphra Behn* (New York: Dial Press, 1980); George Woodcock, *The Incomparable Aphra* (London: T. V. Boardman, 1948). In addition to these works, book-length treatments of Behn in this century include the brief biography by Victoria Sackville-West, *Aphra Behn: The Incomparable Astrea* (New York: Viking, 1928); a historical monograph by William J. Cameron, *New Light on Aphra Behn: An Investigation into the Facts and Fictions Surrounding Her Journey to Surinam in 1663 and Her Activities as a Spy in Flanders in 1666* (Auckland: University of Auckland, 1961); and a Twayne study by Frederick M. Link, *Aphra Behn* (New York: Twayne, 1968).

4. Ernest Bernbaum, "Mrs. Behn's Biography, a Fiction," *PMLA* 28 (1913): 432–53, and "Mrs. Behn's *Oroonoko*," in *Anniversary Papers by Colleagues and Pupils of George Lyman Kittredge* (Boston: Ginn, 1913). For the refutations of Bernbaum's claim that Behn owes her account of Guiana entirely to George Warren's *Impartial Description of Surinam* (1667), see Harrison Grau Platt, "Astrea and Celadon: An Untouched Portrait of Aphra Behn," *PMLA* 49 (1934): 544–59; and especially Goreau, *Reconstructing Aphra*, 41–69.

and her contemporaries. But until very recently, this enterprise of reading Aphra Behn focused on issues such as female self-consciousness, narrative form, or the problem of the woman writer.[5] Feminist criticism has opened up *Oroonoko* to readers who twenty-five years ago would have stuck to Dryden, Rochester, or Congreve. But even though that feminist revision has been significant, productive, and politically necessary—especially for contemporary projects in political criticism such as this book—the recovery of the text of *Oroonoko* was quite unnecessary. In another tradition of cultural criticism apparently inaccessible to the feminist revisionists who "recovered" Behn for students of literature, *Oroonoko* has long held a prominent place. The novella has been recognized as a seminal work in the tradition of antislavery writings from the time of its publication down to our own period. The story of Behn's "royal slave" occupied the English stage for almost a century in dramatic redactions by Thomas Southerne (*Oroonoko*, 1696) and John Hawkesworth (a revision of Southerne's play, 1759). And its sentimental authenticity was confirmed and enhanced by the famous occasion in 1749 when an African "prince" and his companion, previously sold into slavery but ransomed by the British government and received in state in London, attended a performance of Southerne's *Oroonoko*. Affected "with that generous grief which pure nature always feels, and which art had not yet taught them to suppress, the young prince was so far overcome, that he was obliged to retire at the end of the fourth act. His companion remained, but wept the whole time; a circumstance which affected the audience yet more than the play, and

5. Judith Gardiner, "Aphra Behn: Sexuality and Self-Respect," *Women's Studies* 7 (1980): 67–78; William Spengemann, "The Earliest American Novel: Aphra Behn's *Oroonoko*," *Nineteenth-Century Fiction* 38 (1984): 384–414; Larry Carver, "Aphra Behn: The Poet's Heart in a Woman's Body," *Papers on Language and Literature* 14 (1978): 414–24.

doubled the tears which were shed for *Oroonoko* and *Imo-inda*."[6] Historians of slavery have never neglected *Oroonoko*, and in the two most important accounts of literary treatments of slavery that deal with eighteenth-century England, Wylie Sypher's *Guinea's Captive Kings* (1942) and David Brion Davis's *Problem of Slavery in Western Culture* (1966), Oroonoko figures prominently as a significant and even prototypical character in "a vast literature depicting noble African slaves" (*Problem of Slavery*, 473), a crucial early text in the sentimental, antislavery tradition, which grew steadily in frequency and vehemence throughout the eighteenth century.[7]

The feminist recovery of *Oroonoko* largely overlooked the primary concern of Behn's work. Only very recently have issues of slavery and race been addressed by literary critics of Behn, just as these issues have only recently arisen as a focus of concern for new work in eighteenth-century literary culture in general.[8] In both cases, the neglect of race and slavery demonstrates a striking and symptomatic blindness. This is the period of the largest slave trade in history, when at least six million human beings were forcibly transported across the Atlantic to produce a massive new work force on two continents and in the islands of the West Indies. England's participation in the slave trade, especially after the Peace of Utrecht in 1713 and the acquisition of

6. *The Gentleman's Magazine* 19 (16 February 1749), 89–90. See also *The London Magazine* 18 (February 1749), 94. This event is described by David Brion Davis in his *Problem of Slavery in Western Culture* (Ithaca: Cornell University Press, 1966), 477, and by Wylie Sypher in his "African Prince in London," *Journal of the History of Ideas* 2 (1941): 242, among others.

7. Wylie Sypher, *Guinea's Captive Kings: British Anti-Slavery Literature of the XVIIIth Century* (Chapel Hill: University of North Carolina Press, 1942).

8. See the special issue of *Eighteenth-Century Studies* (23 [1990]) edited by Felicity Nussbaum, "The Politics of Difference."

the Asiento—the exclusive right to supply slaves to the West Indies—has been extensively documented.[9] But perhaps more important for literary critics, we have had at our fingertips for over forty years Wylie Sypher's exhaustive description of the pervasive references to slavery in the literature of the period, from William Dodd and Thomas Bellamy to Daniel Defoe and James Thomson. If, in this context, critics in the field were almost universally oblivious to the issue of race until the 1990s, feminist critics only followed suit.

Thus, although *Oroonoko* is certainly a crucial text in the tradition of women's literature and in the development of the novel; although it supplies us with an interesting early example of the problematic stance of a self-consciously female narrator; and although it demonstrates almost programmatically the tensions that arise when romance and realism are brought together, it demands, at this point in our rereading of eighteenth-century literature, a broader political reevaluation. *Oroonoko* can serve as a theoretical test case for the necessary connection of race and gender, a model for the mutual interaction of the positions of the oppressed in the literary discourse of its own age, and a mirror for modern criticism in which one political reading can reflect another, one revisionist school a variety of revisions. Jean-Paul Sartre's juxtaposition in the epigraph to this chapter of "what we have made of them" and "what we have made of ourselves" suggests the reciprocal movement that must form the basis of such a political revisionism, both within the treatment of specific texts and in the discipline of literary studies at large. In Sartre's reading of Frantz Fanon, that reciprocity is the prerequisite for a rela-

9. For example, Richard B. Sheridan, *Sugar and Slavery: An Economic History of the British West Indies, 1623–1775* (Baltimore: Johns Hopkins University Press, 1974), esp. 249–53.

tionship of mutual knowledge between the colonizer and the colonized. In this reading of *Oroonoko*, the figure of the woman in the imperialist narrative—a sign of "what we have made of ourselves"—provides the point of contact through which the violence of colonial history—"what we have made of them"—can be represented.

Indeed, juxtaposing race and gender in the study of ideology and literary culture might seem almost automatic, since recent work on postcolonial and third-world literature has depended so strongly on the very analytical category that underwrites much contemporary feminist theory: the notion of the "other." The staging of the relationship of alterity has taken many forms in contemporary theory. Beginning perhaps with the scenario derived from Hegel of the paradigmatic play between master and slave, the "other" in contemporary theory can be internalized as a dimension of the psychological dynamic, or externalized as an account of social forms and structures. Feminist critics have drawn widely and eclectically from the interconnected dualisms that arise from deploying the category of the "other" to describe the position of women in patriarchal culture. More recently, third-world critics have utilized the category of the "other" to explore the relationship of colonizer and colonized, Occident and Orient, European and native, white and black. But with the exception of Gayatri Chakravorty Spivak, neither group has used the concurrence of terms as the occasion for combining these critiques. The force of Spivak's work, in this context, has been in her insistence on the distortions that occur when a feminist approach fails to recognize colonialism and, reciprocally, in her reading of the literary culture of colonizer and colonized through the figure of the woman.[10] For most

10. Gayatri Chakravorty Spivak, *In Other Worlds: Essays in Cultural Politics* (New York: Routledge, 1988).

of the recent critics of colonial and neocolonial literature, however, gender enters not at all into the analysis of colonialist ideology. Such a striking irony is perhaps symptomatic of a constraint implicit in these dualisms—a binary logic that militates against the dialectical argument at which this essay aims.

In addition to forestalling the conjunction of critical accounts of race and gender and thus the alignment and interaction of political readings, the notion of the "other" also works to hold apart the historical categories of imperialist and native. This dualism is in part the inevitable accompaniment to a politically necessary polarization, a polarization that enables Edward Said to detail the massive and diffuse spectrum of discursive power controlled by the colonizer, and that gives Frantz Fanon a powerful terminology in which to advocate revolutionary struggle. For Said "Orientalism" is a discourse of power, a "distribution of geopolitical awareness" into various cultural forms—"aesthetic, scholarly, economic, sociological, historical, and philological"—by which the Occident creates and concurrently intends to understand, "control, manipulate, even to incorporate" the Oriental "other."[11] *Orientalism*, then, documents and demystifies the discourse of the Occident from the perspective of the third world, just as, from the same perspective but with the alternative strategy, Fanon's writings articulate the interests of the colonized, recounting, theorizing, and ultimately advocating a struggle to the death, through the absolute and violent conflict in the colonial world between settler and native.[12]

Following Fanon, Abdul JanMohamed provides perhaps the clearest model for the role of the "other" in the critique

11. Edward W. Said, *Orientalism* (New York: Random House, 1979), 13.
12. See Frantz Fanon, *The Wretched of the Earth*, trans. Constance Farrington (New York: Grove Press, 1968).

of colonialism. In *Manichean Aesthetics* and elsewhere, Jan-Mohamed argues that "the dominant model of power-and interest-relations in all colonial societies is the manichean opposition between the putative superiority of the European and the supposed inferiority of the native."[13] Despite the claim to a dialectical argument, this binary opposition represents an aesthetic version of the manichean historical struggle described by Fanon. For JanMohamed, attention to imperialist practices reveals the typical structure of colonialist ideology and literary culture, its constitution by a choice of identity with or difference from the "other." And Tzvetan Todorov, in his account of "the conquest of America"—an account, in his words, of "the discovery the *self* makes of the *other*"[14]—depends, perhaps more systematically than any other critic of colonialism, upon the argument from alterity. For Todorov, Columbus, like "every colonist in his relations to the colonized," conceives of the native according to the "two component parts" of alterity, which are absolute identity and absolute difference (*Conquest of America* 42).

Said, Fanon, JanMohamed, and Todorov locate the "other" extrinsically, in the historical struggle—ideological, political, and revolutionary—between the colonizer and the native. Homi Bhabha focuses instead upon an intrinsic otherness within the colonial subject that operates as a pressure, a repetition, or a mutation, like the difference between a self and its doubles. In Bhabha's scheme, the dominant discourse of colonialism produces this difference when it attempts to represent the native; at that point, inevitably, "other 'denied' knowledges enter upon the dominant

---

13. Abdul JanMohamed, *Manichean Aesthetics: The Politics of Literature in Colonial Africa* (Amherst: University of Massachusetts Press, 1983), and "The Economy of Manichean Allegory: The Function of Racial Difference in Colonialist Literature," *Critical Inquiry* 12 (1985): 63.

14. Tzvetan Todorov, *The Conquest of America: The Question of the Other*, trans. Richard Howard (New York: Harper & Row, 1984), 4.

discourse and estrange the basis of its authority."[15] Thus although Bhabha argues directly against a "power struggle between self and Other, or . . . mother culture and alien cultures" ("Signs Taken for Wonders" 153), he does posit within the colonial subject an unresolvable division that in effect reproduces the dualism described by Said, JanMohamed, and Todorov.

Bhabha's position raises the problem of the status of opposition for some of the critics who adopt the perspective of alterity. At some points it appears that Bhabha argues that the only autonomy remaining for the native "other" resides within the dominant colonial discourse, since, in Bhabha's view, colonizer and colonized both participate in the complex problematic of colonial identity through which difference is incorporated by power. Though Bhabha does claim that "the discursive conditions of dominance [turn] into the grounds of intervention" ("Signs Taken for Wonders" 154), the force of his argument tends to suggest that opposition is contained within the production of colonial power. This notion of the pervasive, preemptive nature of power is most often evoked by "new historicist" critics and is perhaps most clearly defined by Stephen Greenblatt in an essay on Shakespeare's second *Henriad*. Discussing the "alien voices," the "alien interpretations" encountered by the first English settlers in Virginia, Greenblatt claims that "subversiveness, as I have argued, was produced by the colonial power in its own interest."[16] Here the category of the "other" foregrounds and privileges the position of power,

---

15. Homi K. Bhabha, "Signs Taken for Wonders: Questions of Ambivalence and Authority under a Tree Outside Delhi, May 1817," *Critical Inquiry* 12 (1985): 156. See also his "Other Question—The Stereotype and Colonial Discourse," *Screen* 24 (1983): 18–36.

16. Stephen Greenblatt, "Invisible Bullets: Renaissance Authority and Its Subversion, *Henry IV* and *Henry V*," in *Political Shakespeare: New Essays in Cultural Materialism*, ed. Jonathan Dollimore and Alan Sinfield (Ithaca: Cornell University Press, 1985), 24.

and concurrently functions to minimize or eliminate the notion of an active or autonomous resistance, and sometimes of any opposition at all.

Productive and important as it has been for these critics of colonialism, the category of the "other" seems nevertheless to have stymied systematically the possibility of a dialectical critique of colonial culture. It forecloses an approach that works through alterity to the mutual interaction between positions of oppression. And it sometimes also precludes finding a place for the voice and the struggles of the native even in the massive and complex edifices of power that seem to surround and contain all resistance. But the ideal of an argument that moves beyond absolute difference has been raised repeatedly as a utopian image by many recent critics. Todorov ends with the hopeful assertion that "self-knowledge develops through knowledge of the Other" (*Conquest of America* 254). He seeks ultimately to locate a position beyond difference: "We need not be confined within a sterile alternative: either to justify colonial wars (in the name of the superiority of Western civilization), or to reject all interaction with a foreign power in the name of one's own identity. Nonviolent communication exists, and we can defend it as a value" (182). JanMohamed too imagines a "syncretic possibility," theoretically available through the dialectic upon which his manichean opposition is founded, but present in practice only as an unrealized negative example ("Economy of Manichean Allegory" 65), symptomatic of the difficulty of transcending alterity. In the same way, Said turns to the "human" at the end of *Orientalism*: "I consider Orientalism's failure to have been a human as much as an intellectual one; for in having to take up a position of irreducible opposition to a region of the world it considered alien to its own, Orientalism failed to identify with human experience, failed also to see it as human experience." "Without 'the Orient' there would be scholars, critics, intellectuals, human beings, for whom the racial, ethnic, and national distinctions were less important than the common enterprise of promoting human community" (328). "Communication," "syncretic possibility," "human community"—however it is named, this gesture outside the "other" is at best an adjunctive, utopian moment, attractive but obviously extraneous to the argument from alterity. It gives us a sentiment without a method, and we can derive from these examples our inspiration, but not our critical practice.

My treatment of *Oroonoko* is extensively indebted to the critics I have described above, but in it I seek to avoid what I see as the theoretical pitfalls of the "other," and to substitute a dialectical notion of mutual interaction, a category that Johannes Fabian, in a critique of modern anthropological writing, calls "radical contemporaneity."[17] Focusing on the use of time as a distancing mechanism, Fabian offers a critique of the way in which modern anthropology constructs the relationship between the knower and the known, the anthropologist and the native. Temporalizations placing the native in the "primitive" past or in a "passage from savagery to civilization, from peasant to industrial society" (*Time and the Other* 95) have constituted the discipline since its inception, and Fabian argues that this systematic "denial of coevalness" (31) has operated in the ideological service of colonialism and neocolonialism. These temporalizations conceal the fact that "anthropology's Other is, ultimately, other people who are our contemporaries" (143). Fabian proposes that anthropologists "seek ways to meet the Other on the same ground, in the same Time" (164). His notion of radical contemporaneity is based on the Marxian theory of history as embodied in the

17. Johannes Fabian, *Time and the Other: How Anthropology Makes Its Object* (New York: Columbia University Press, 1983), xi.

formations of the present, on a view of "the totality of historical forces, including their cotemporality at any given
time" (158). Marx's "radical presentism" (159) allowed him
to formulate a theory of political economy, and it can allow
the discipline of anthropology to perceive itself as part of
an historical present in which its own activity is part of what
it studies (157). In this sense, radical contemporaneity
serves "as the condition for truly dialectical confrontation
between persons as well as societies. It militates against false
conceptions of dialectics—all those watered-down binary
abstractions which are passed off as oppositions: left vs.
right, past vs. present, primitive vs. modern . . . . What are
opposed, in conflict, in fact, locked in antagonistic struggle,
are not the same societies at different stages of development, but different societies facing each other at the same
Time" (155). For Fabian "the anthropologist and his inter-
locutors only 'know' when they meet each other in one and
the same cotemporality" (164). The critic of literary culture
can rarely argue that the colonialist author and his characters "meet the Other on the same ground, in the same
Time." But if we read from the perspective of radical contemporaneity, we can seek in the texts of colonialism signs
of the dialectical confrontations embodied in the historical
formations of this colonial period. And though the colonialist and the native never fully "know" each other, or
their common historical present, we can perhaps, by this
means, come to know something of both.

   The aim of this critical project, then, is not simply to re-
read the problem of race, or the problem of gender, or the
problem of race and gender considered as two independent lines of inquiry, but rather to demonstrate the contemporaneity of issues of race and gender in the context of
a particular stage in the history of British capitalism associated broadly with commodity exchange and colonialist
exploitation. Obviously, other theoretical paradigms, and

even other relations of oppression, might usefully be brought to bear here and elsewhere. But the issues of gender and race are crucially connected in this particular text, and, more broadly, their conjunction here is sufficient to demonstrate the value of a pragmatic dialectical criticism, and indeed the political importance of refusing to posit any opposition as absolute.

Oroonoko seems at first to be a rather recalcitrant model for "radical contemporaneity": the novella lends itself with greater readiness to the argument from alterity. Indeed, Behn's opening description of Oroonoko, the "royal slave," is a locus classicus of the trope of sentimental identification by which the native "other" is naturalized as a European aristocrat. In physical appearance, the narrator can barely distinguish her native prince from those of England:

> [Oroonoko] was pretty tall, but of a Shape the most exact that can be fancy'd: The most famous Statuary cou'd not form the Figure of a Man more admirably turn'd from head to foot. . . . His Nose was rising and *Roman*, instead of *African* and flat. His Mouth the finest shaped that could be seen; far from those great turn'd Lips, which are so natural to the rest of the Negroes. The whole Proportion and Air of his Face was so nobly and exactly form'd, that bating his Colour, there could be nothing in Nature more beautiful, agreeable and Handsome. (*Oroonoko* 8)

If this account of Oroonoko's classical European beauty makes it possible to forget his race, the narrator's description of his character and accomplishments further elaborates the act of absolute identity through which he is initially represented:

> Nor did the Perfections of his Mind come short of those of his Person; and whoever had heard him speak, wou'd have

been convinced of their Errors, that all fine Wit is confined to
the white Men, especially to those of Christendom. . . .

'twas amazing to imagine . . . where 'twas he got that real
Greatness of Soul, those refined Notions of true Honour, that
absolute Generosity, and that Softness that was capable of the
highest Passions of Love and Gallantry. . . . the most illus-
trious Courts could not have produced a braver Man, both
for Greatness of Courage and Mind, a Judgment more solid,
a Wit more quick, and a Conversation more sweet and diverting. He knew almost as much as if he had read much: He had
heard of and admired the *Romans*: He had heard of the late
Civil Wars in *England*, and the deplorable Death of our great
Monarch; and wou'd discourse of it with all the Sense and
Abhorrence of the Injustice imaginable. He had an extreme
good and graceful Mien, and all the Civility of a well-bred
great Man. He had nothing of Barbarity in his Nature, but in
all Points address'd himself as if his Education had been in
some *European* Court. (8, 7)

Oroonoko is not only a natural European and aristocrat,
but a natural neoclassicist and Royalist as well, an absurdity
generated by the desire for an intimate identification with
the "royal slave." Like Columbus in Todorov's account,
Behn's narrator seems to have only two choices within the
frame of alterity: either to conceive the "other" as absolutely different from and necessarily inferior to herself, or
to see him as identical, fully assimilable to her own mirror
image. "Difference is corrupted into inequality, equality
into identity. These are the two great figures of the relation
to the other that delimit the other's inevitable space"
(Todorov, *Conquest of America*, 146); inevitable because, in
JanMohamed's words, any other relation to alterity would
require the bracketing of one's own culture, "in practice the
virtually impossible task of negating one's very being, precisely because one's culture is what formed that being"

("Economy of Manichean Allegory" 65). The obvious mystification involved in Behn's depiction of Oroonoko as a European aristocrat in blackface does not necessarily damage the novella's emancipationist reputation; precisely this kind of sentimental identification was in fact the staple component of antislavery narratives in England and America for the next century and a half. But the failure of Behn's novella to see beyond the mirror of its own culture in this opening characterization of its hero raises the question of the nature of Behn's relationship with the African slave.

The action of *Oroonoko* forces us to repeat that question at every turn; not only is the novella's protagonist an aristocratic hero, but his story is largely constructed in the tradition of heroic romance. Briefly, Oroonoko, a noble African prince, falls in love with Imoinda, the daughter of his aristocratic foster-father. The two are divided first by the intervention of the King, Oroonoko's grandfather, who covets Imoinda for himself, and then by their independent sale into slavery. Reunited in Suriname, the British colony in Guiana where Behn was a visitor, Oroonoko and Imoinda are at first promised their freedom, then lead a slave rebellion, and finally die—Imoinda at the hands of Oroonoko, Oroonoko (known by the slave name of Caesar) executed by the colonists. Oroonoko's exploits follow quite closely the pattern outlined by Eugene Waith for the "Herculean hero," the superhuman epic protagonist who plays a major role in heroic form from the classical period through the Renaissance.[18] He is invincible in battle, doing single-handedly "such things as will not be believed that Human Strength could perform" (*Oroonoko* 30). He is also a man of wit and address, governed absolutely by his allegiance to the conventional aristocratic code of love and honor. When

18. Eugene M. Waith, *The Herculean Hero in Marlowe, Chapman, Shakespeare, and Dryden* (New York: Columbia University Press, 1962).

he declares his love to Imoinda, for instance, it is voiced entirely in the familiar terms of heroic romance: "Most happily, some new, and, till then, unknown Power instructed his Heart and Tongue in the Language of Love . . . . his Flame aim'd at nothing but Honour, if such a distinction may be made in Love" (10).

This formula is typical of the dramatic redactions of heroic romance by Davenant, Orrery, Dryden, and Lee that were prominent on the English stage from the Restoration through the 1670s and, in a weaker form, beyond. As a dramatist, Behn had herself contributed to this genre in *Abdelazer*, a heroic tragedy produced and published in 1677. We can trace the use of heroic convention in *Oroonoko*, then, directly to the aristocratic coterie theater of the Restoration. One of the tropes of this form is apparent in the language in which Oroonoko swears his loyalty to "his charming Imoinda" (71):

> they mutually protested, that even Fetters and Slavery were soft and easy, and would be supported with Joy and Pleasure, while they cou'd be so happy to possess each other, and to be able to make good their Vows. *Caesar* swore he disdained the Empire of the World, while he could behold his *Imoinda*. (44)

This abdication of empire for love is one of the persistent motifs of late heroic drama, exemplified most prominently by Dryden's Anthony in *All for Love* (1677): "Give to your boy, your Caesar, / This rattle of a globe to play withal, / . . . . / I'll not be pleased with less than Cleopatra."[19]

The conventions of heroic romance include perhaps the most powerfully hierarchical and rigid literary system available in late Restoration England, a factor directly pertinent to their relevance in the representation of the alien and

19. John Dryden, *All for Love*, ed. David Vieth (Lincoln: University of Nebraska Press, 1972), II.442–46.

unfamiliar scenes of West Indian slavery. In a discussion of nineteenth-century travel writing, Mary Louise Pratt analyzes various discursive strategies that the imperialist observer uses to textualize, contain, and process the alien figure of the native. She defines this phenomenon as "reductive normalizing," a textual device which she finds to be typical of writing about the imperial frontier "where Europeans confront not only unfamiliar Others but unfamiliar selves," and where "they engage in not just the reproduction of the capitalist mode of production but its expansion through displacement of previously established modes."[20] In Behn's text the work of "reductive normalizing," this process of familiarization and codification gauged to "mediate the shock of contact on the frontier" (Pratt, "Scratches," 121), is carried out through literary convention, and specifically through that very convention most effectively able to fix and codify the experience of radical alterity, the arbitrary codes of love and honor found in heroic romance.

Emerging directly from this heroic mystification is the persistent presence of the figure of the woman in the discourse and action of *Oroonoko*. In the ideology of heroic romance, of course, the desirable woman serves invariably as the motive and the ultimate prize for male adventures. As this ideology evolved in the seventeenth-century French prose tradition dominated by women writers such as Madeleine de Scudery and Madame de LaFayette, women became increasingly central to the romantic action. Behn's novellas, like other English prose works of the Restoration and early eighteenth century, draw extensively upon this French material, and the foregrounding of female authorship in *Oroonoko* through the explicit interventions of the

20. Mary Louise Pratt, "Scratches on the Face of the Country; or, What Mr. Barrow Saw in the Land of the Bushmen," *Critical Inquiry* 12 (1985): 121.

female narrator signal the prevalent feminization of the genre.

This narrative must have women, and it generates—or rather ingeminates—female figures at every turn, as observers, beneficiaries, and consumers of Oroonoko's romantic action. Not only is the protagonist represented as especially fond of the company of women (*Oroonoko* 46), but female figures—either Imoinda or the narrator and her surrogates—appear as incentives or witnesses for almost all of Oroonoko's exploits. In the compact account of his heroic contests, he fights a monstrous, purportedly immortal tiger for the romantic approval of his female admirers: "*What Trophies and Garlands, Ladies, will you make me, if I bring you home the Heart of this ravenous Beast . . . ? We all promis'd he should be rewarded at all our hands*" (51). He kills the first tiger in defense of a group of four women—who "fled as fast as we could" (50)—and an unidentified, symptomatically faceless Englishman, who effaces himself further by fleeing with the ladies (50). On the trip—over which Oroonoko presides as expedition leader—to the Indian tribes, the female figure is again the center of attention. Along with the narrator and her "Woman, a Maid of good Courage" (54), only one man agrees to accompany Oroonoko to the Indian town, and once there, the "*White* people," surrounded by the naked natives, stage a scene of cultural difference in which the fully clothed woman is the central spectacle:

They were all naked; and we were dress'd . . . very glittering and rich; so that we appear'd extremely fine: my own Hair was cut short, and I had a taffety Cap, with black Feathers on my Head . . . . from gazing upon us round, they touch'd us, laying their Hands upon all the Features of our Faces, feeling our Breasts and Arms, taking up one Petticoat, then wondering to see another; admiring our Shoes and Stockings, but

more our Garters, which we gave 'em, and they ty'd about
their Legs. (55)

So ubiquitous and apparently essential is the female eye in
the novella that even at the scene of Oroonoko's death, the
narrator unobtrusively informs us that, though she was absent, "my Mother and Sister were by him" (77).

The narrator herself, in her account of her position as
the female author of Oroonoko's story, makes it even more
evident that the romantic hero is the production and expression of a female sensibility, just as his story is a production of "only a Female Pen" (40). The narrator's act of
modest self-effacement here, and again on the last page of
the novella, is a signal of the special relevance she claims
for the female figure as author, character, and ultimate arbiter of Oroonoko's romance, in contrast to the "sublime"
masculine wit that would have omitted the crucial naturalness and simplicity (1) of the tale for which the female pen
has an innate affinity:

> Thus died this great Man, worthy of a better Fate, and a
> more sublime Wit than mine to write his Praise: Yet, I hope,
> the Reputation of my pen is considerable enough to make his
> glorious Name to survive to all Ages, with that of the brave,
> the beautiful, and the constant *Imoinda*. (78)

As the female narrator, along with the proliferation of female characters who serve as her proxies, produces Oroonoko's heroic drama, so that they become in turn its consumers, Oroonoko also, on the same model and because of
his proximity to the female, is represented as a consumer
of the romantic form he enacts. He keeps company with
the women in the colony, in preference to the men, and in
their conversations he and Imoinda are "entertained . . .
with the Loves of the *Romans*" (46), a pastime that inciden-
tally serves to forestall Oroonoko's complaints about his

captivity. In the end, then, even Oroonoko himself is feminized, incorporated into the circular system by which the
figure of the woman becomes both object and beneficiary
of romantic form.

We must now move, with the help of history, away from
the romantic "normalization" that provides the narrative
paradigm of *Oroonoko*. Needless to say, the model of heroic
romance does not account for all the material in Behn's
representation of West Indian slavery. In fact, neither the
theme of slavery nor the romantic action explain the extended description of the Caribs, the native Americans of
Guiana, with which Behn begins. This opening description
deploys another set of discursive conventions and opens
another range of ideological expectations than those of romance. The natives are the novella's noble savages, absolutely innocent and without sin, immodesty, or fraud. The
notion of natural innocence, which civilization and laws can
only destroy, is obviously incompatible with the hierarchical
aristocratic ideology of heroic form; Oroonoko, educated
by a Frenchman, is admirable for his connection with—not
his distance from—European civilization. The account of
the Indians belongs in part to the tradition of travel narratives, by Behn's period an established and widely popular
mode describing voyages and colonial expeditions to the
new world and including detailed reports of marvels, which
range from accurate botanical and ethnographic records to
pure invention.[21]

Behn's opening account of the Indians establishes her

21. In the earlier period, Richard Haklyut's *Principall Navigations* (London, 1589) and Samuel Purchas's *Hakluytus Posthumus; or, Purchas His Pilgrimes* (London, 1616); in the later period, Sir Hans Sloane's *Voyage to the
Islands Madera, Barbados, Nieves, S. Christophers and Jamaica* . . . (London,
1707) and Charles Churchill's *Collection of Voyages and Travels* (London,
1732).

credibility in this context, but in its almost exclusive emphasis on trade with the natives, it also indicates the economic backdrop of the history of the "royal slave":

> Trading with them for their Fish, Venison, Buffalo's Skins, and little Rarities; as *Marmosets . . . Cousheries . . . .* Then for little *Paraketoes*, great *Parrots*, *Muckaws*, and a thousand other Birds and Beasts of wonderful and surprizing Forms and Colours. For Skins of prodigious Snakes . . . also some rare Flies, of amazing Forms and Colours . . . Then we trade for Feathers, which they order into all Shapes, make themselves little short Habits of 'em, and glorious Wreaths for their Heads, Necks, Arms and Legs, whose Tinctures are unconceivable. I had a Set of these presented to me, and I gave 'em to the King's Theatre, and it was the Dress of the *Indian Queen*, infinitely admired by Persons of Quality; and was unimitable. Besides these, a thousand little Knacks, and Rarities in Nature; and some of Art, as their Baskets, Weapons, Aprons . . . . (2)

The marvels here are all movable objects, readily transportable to a European setting, where they become exotic and desirable acquisitions. Behn's enumeration of these goods belongs to a widespread discourse of imperialist accumulation, typical of both the economic and the literary language of the Restoration and early eighteenth century, in which the mere act of proliferative listing, the evocation of brilliant colors, and the sense of an incalculable quantity express the period's fascination with imperialist acquisition.[22] But the Indians' goods are at best a small factor in the real economic connection between England and the West Indies; they serve primarily as a synechdoche for imperialist exploitation.

22. See my *Alexander Pope* (Oxford: Basil Blackwell, 1985), chap. 1.

This opening moment of economic and historical contextualization centers around the feathered habit that the narrator acquires, and which, she claims, became upon her return to England the dress of the Indian Queen in Dryden's heroic play of the same name (1664), an artifact of imperialism displayed in the most spectacular manner possible—adorning the female figure of a contemporary actress on the real stage of the Theatre Royal in Bridges Street. This foregrounding of female dress recalls that scene of the expedition to the Indian village, in which the spectacle of the narrator's clothing is similarly privileged. And in general, these items in the opening account of imperialist trade are meant to reflect the acquisitive instincts of a specifically female sensibility—dress, skins, and exotic pets. Pets, indeed, in particular birds, were both sign and product of the expansion and commercialization of English economy and society in the eighteenth century.[23] But this expansion and commercialization found its most frequent cultural emblem in the figure of the woman. Female dress and ornamentation—perfumes, pearls, jewels, silks, combs, petticoats—and the female territory of the tea table with its imported essentials of coffee, tea, and chocolate—came to stand for trade, prosperity, luxury, and commodification in a characteristic synecdoche that pervades the literary culture of this period from Defoe and Rowe to Pope and Swift.[24] And this connection leads to the metonymical association of women, even unadorned, with the ideologically complex phenomenon of mercantile capitalism: goods for female consump-

23. J. H. Plumb, "The Acceptance of Modernity," in Neil McKendrick, John Brewer, and J. H. Plumb, *The Birth of a Consumer Society: The Commercialization of Eighteenth-Century England* (Bloomington: Indiana University Press, 1982), 321–22.

24. See Neil McKendrick, "The Commercialization of Fashion," in McKendrick, Brewer, and Plumb, *The Birth of a Consumer Society*, esp. 51.

tion and then women in general come to stand for the massive historical, economic, and social enterprise of English imperialism.

And here, of course, the substantial trade, and the real profit, was not in these exotic objects for female consumption—buffalo skins, *Paraketoes*, or feathers—but in sugar and slaves. Behn's description of the slave trade, highly accurate in many of its details, is the shaping economic and historical context of *Oroonoko*. A letter written in 1663 to Sir Robert Harley, at whose house at St. John's Hill the narrator claims to have resided (49), from one William Yearworth, his steward, may describe the arrival of the slave ship which Behn would have witnessed during her visit to the colony:[25]

> Theare is A genney man [a slave ship from the Guinea Coast] Ariued heare in This riuer of ye 24th of [January] This Instant att Sande poynt. Shee hase 130 nigroes one Borde; ye Comanders name [is] Joseph John Woode; shee has lost 54 negroes in ye viage. The Ladeyes that are heare liue att St Johnes hill.[26]

Behn recounts the participation of the African tribal leaders in collecting and selling slaves to European traders, the prearranged agreements for lots in the colonies, the deliberate dispersal of members of the same tribe around the plantations, the situation of the Negro towns, the imminence of rebellion, and—as we shall subsequently see—the aggressive character of the Koromantyn (in Behn, Cora-

---

25. See Goreau, *Reconstructing Aphra*, 56.
26. "Letters to Sir Robert Harley from the Stewards of His Plantations in Surinam. (1663–4)," reprinted in *Colonising Expeditions to the West Indies and Guiana, 1623–1667*, ed. V. T. Harlow (London: Hakluyt Society, 1925), 90.

mantien) slaves, the name given to slaves sold at the Gold Coast trading sites from which Oroonoko comes.[27]

Though the uprising Behn recounts—an obvious consequence of the slave trade—has no specific historical counterpart, the situation she presents is typical. Revolts and runaways, or maroons, were commonplace in the West Indies and Guiana throughout this period. In Jamaica rebellions and guerilla warfare, predominantly led by Koromantyn ex-slaves, were virtually continuous from 1665 to 1740.[28] Marronage was common in Guiana as well during the period in which *Oroonoko* is set. In fact, while Behn was in Suriname a group of escaped slaves led by a Koromantyn known as Jermes had an established base in the region of Para, from which they attacked local plantations (Price, *Guiana Maroons*, 23). Wylie Sypher has documented several cases similar to Oroonoko's, in which the offspring of African tribal leaders were betrayed into slavery, often on their way to obtain an education in England ("African Prince in London").

The powerful act of "reductive normalizing" performed by the romantic narrative is countered, then, at least in part, by a similarly powerful historical contextualization that we can observe in Behn's account of trade. Not that the representation of trade in *Oroonoko* is outside ideology; far from it. We have already seen the position implicitly assigned to women in Behn's account of imperialist accumulation to be profoundly connected with the mechanisms

27. *Koromantyn* or *Coromantijn* is a name derived from the Dutch fort at Koromantyn on the Gold Coast; in Suriname it designated slaves from the Fanti, Ashanti, and other interior Gold Coast tribes. For background and statistics on the tribal origins of the Bush Negroes of Guiana, see Richard Price, *The Guiana Maroons: A Historical and Bibliographical Introduction* (Baltimore: Johns Hopkins University Press, 1976), 12–16.

28. Orlando Patterson, "Slavery and Slave Revolts: A Sociohistorical Analysis of the First Maroon War, 1665–1740," in *Maroon Societies: Rebel Slave Communities in the Americas*, ed. Richard Price, 2 ed. (Baltimore: Johns Hopkins University Press, 1979), esp. 256–70.

by which the expansionist impulses of mercantile capitalism were deferred and rationalized; and we could also examine the novella's assumption, partly produced by the crossover from the code of romantic honor, that blacks captured in war are legitimate objects for the slave trade. We cannot read Behn's version of colonialist history uncritically, any more than we can her heroic romance. But we can read them together, because they are oriented around the same governing point of reference, the ubiquitous and indispensable figure of the woman. In the paradigm of heroic romance, women are the objects and arbiters of male adventurism, just as, in the ideology of imperialist accumulation, women are the emblems and proxies of the whole male enterprise of colonialism. The female narrator and her proliferative surrogates serve as the enabling point of contact between romance and trade in *Oroonoko*, motivating the hero's exploits, validating his romantic appeal, and witnessing his tragic fate. Simultaneously they dress themselves in the products of imperialist acquisition, enacting the colonialist paradigm of exploitation and consumption, not only of the Indians' feathers and skins, and the many marvels of the new world, but of slaves as well, and the adventure of the "royal slave" himself.

We can see these two paradigms intersecting in Oroonoko's anti-slavery speech:

> *And why* (said he) *my dear Friends and Fellow-sufferers, should we be Slaves to an unknown People? Have they vanquished us nobly in Fight? Have they won us in Honourable Battle? And are we by the Chance of War become their Slaves? This wou'd not anger a noble Heart; this would not animate a Soldier's Soul: no, but we are bought and sold like Apes or Monkeys, to be the sport of Women, Fools and Cowards.* (61)

The attack on slavery is voiced in part through the codes of heroic romance: the trade in slaves is unjust only if and when slaves are not honorably conquered in battle. But these lines also allude to the other ideology of *Oroonoko*, the feminization of trade that we have associated primarily with the depiction of the Indians. Oroonoko's resentment at being "bought and sold like Apes or Monkeys . . . the sport of women" seems less unprovoked given the prominent opening description of the animals and birds traded by the Indians, in particular the little "Marmosets, a sort of Monkey, as big as a Rat or Weasel, but of a marvellous and delicate shape, having Face and Hands like a Human Creature" (2). In conjunction with the image of the pet monkey, Oroonoko's critique of slavery alludes to one of the most powerful redactions of the critique of colonialist ideology—the representation of female consumption, of monkeys and men.

In grounding the parallel systems of romance and trade, the female figure in Behn's novella plays a role like that outlined by Myra Jehlen in an essay on "the paradox of feminist criticism," the role of "Archimedes' lever"—which paradoxically could move the earth, if only it could have a place to stand.[29] Because they are marginal and subordinate to men, women have no extrinsic perspective, no objective status, in this narrative, either as the arbiters of romance or as the beneficiaries of colonialism. They have no place to stand. But in their mediatory role, between heroic romance and mercantile imperialism, they generate and enable the mutual interaction of these two otherwise incompatible discourses. They provide the occasion for the superimposition of aristocratic and bourgeois systems—the ideological contradiction that dominates the novella. And in that contradiction we can locate a site beyond alterity, a point of critique and sympathy effectually produced by the radical

29. Myra Jehlen, "Archimedes and the Paradox of Feminist Criticism," in *The "Signs" Reader: Women, Gender and Scholarship*, ed. Elizabeth Abel and Emily K. Abel (Chicago: University of Chicago Press, 1983), 69–75.

contemporaneity of issues of gender with those of romance and race.

On the face of it, the treatment of slavery in *Oroonoko* is neither coherent nor fully critical. The romance motifs in Oroonoko's story, based upon the elitist focus on the fate of African "princes," render ambiguous Behn's attack on the institution of slavery, and open the way for the development of the sentimental antislavery position of the eighteenth century. But at the same time, the representation of trade and consumption, readily extended to the trade in slaves and the consumption of Oroonoko himself, and specifically imagined through a female sensibility, tends to render colonialism unambiguously attractive. This incoherence in the novella's treatment of slavery can be felt at various points in the course of the narrative. The question of the enslavement of the Indians poses an obvious problem. In the opening trading scene, the colonists are described as living "in perfect Amity" with the Indians, "without daring to command 'em; but, on the contrary, caress 'em with all the brotherly and friendly Affection in the world" (*Oroonoko* 1–2). Indeed, Indians in this area made such uncooperative and unprofitable slaves that the early attempts to enslave them were soon abandoned. This relationship of "amity," then, reflects a pragmatic rather than a "brotherly" commitment to native liberty for the noble savages. And in fact later in the novella the narrator evokes a quite unbrotherly dispute that calls that opening gesture of "friendly Affection" as well as the accompanying category of the noble savage strikingly into question:

About this time we were in many mortal Fears, about some Disputes the *English* had with the *Indians*; so that we could scarce trust our selves, without great Numbers, to go to any *Indian* Towns or Place where they abode, for fear they should

> fall upon us, as they did immediately after my coming away; and the Place being in the Possession of the *Dutch*, they us'd them not so civilly as the *English*: so that they cut in pieces all they could take, getting into Houses, and hanging up the Mother, and all her Children about her; and cut a Footman, I left behind me, all in Joints, and nail'd him to Trees. (54)

This scene of dismemberment gives a visceral dimension to the instability of those assertions of "amity" and "friendship." Indeed, dismemberment and mutilation pervade the novella's relation with the native "other"—both Indian and African. Aside from Oroonoko's own death in the last pages of the novella, and his execution of Imoinda in which he "first [cut] her Throat, and then [severed] her yet smiling Face from that delicate Body" (72), the visit to the Indian town is marked by an account of racial difference defined by this same figure of violence:

> so frightful a Vision it was to see 'em, no Fancy can create; no sad Dreams can represent so dreadful a Spectacle. For my part, I took 'em for Hobgoblins, or Fiends, rather than Men: . . . some wanted their Noses, some their Lips, some both Noses and Lips, some their Ears, and others cut through each Cheek, with long Slashes, through which their Teeth appear'd . . . They told us . . . That when any War was waging, two Men . . . were to stand in competition for the Generalship . . . and being brought before the old Judges . . . they are ask'd, What they dare do, to shew they are worthy to lead an Army? When he who is first ask'd, making no reply, cuts off his Nose, and throws it contemptibly on the ground; the other does something to himself that he thinks surpasses him, and perhaps deprives himself of Lips and an Eye: so they slash on till one gives out, and many have dy'd in this Debate. (57–58)

These passages place the noble savage and the heroic slave together in a position of absolute alterity defined by spectacular brutality, a position with which the category of amity, the attack on slavery, and even the process of "reductive normalizing" are violently contradictory. Indeed, this narrative fascination with dismemberment suggests a perverse connection between the female narrator and Oroonoko's brutal executioners: her stance as an advocate for the "royal slave" is symptomatically unstable.

Despite her asserted sympathy for Oroonoko, the narrator plays a dubious role in the course of his negotiations with the planters for his release. She accepts the task of "diverting" him with romantic tales so that he will continue to believe the planters' promise that he is to be returned to Africa, a promise that she knows to be a ruse (45–46); she seems to collude in the assignment of spies to attend him in his meetings with the other slaves (60); and she speaks for the planters in threatening him with "Confinement" (46) in an attempt to keep him from fomenting rebellion. This performance, like her unexplained absence at the death of her hero, can only be understood as an effect of the text's ideological instability on the topic of slavery.

But beyond these multiple ambiguities, at the climactic moment in the ideological contradiction that dominates the novella, resides a deeper critique of slavery. This insight originates in the hidden contemporary political referent of the narrative: the party quarrels current in the colonies of the West Indies and Guiana at the time of Behn's visit. Though the account supplied in the novella is sketchy at best, Behn names persons whom we can now identify, and animosities that we can now trace to the political tensions that emigrated to the colonies during the English revolution and after the time of the Restoration.[30] As a locus of

30. For details on the political issues in Suriname in the 1660s, see the documents reprinted under "Guiana" in the Hakluyt Society's *Colonising Expeditions to the West Indies and Guiana, 1623–1667*, esp. "The Discription of Guyana," "To y^c Right Honourable y^c Lords of His Majesties most Honorable Privy Councel, The Case of y^c Proscripts from Surinam wth all Humility is briefely but most truely stated. 1662," and "Letters to Sir Rob-

relative political neutrality, the colonies of the West Indies and Guiana attracted Royalists during the revolution, as the king's cause began to weaken in England, and Parliamentarians and radicals after the Restoration—especially those fleeing from prosecution at home. The narrator's rendering of the colonists' council (69), and her account of the contests for jurisdiction over Oroonoko, both before and after his rebellion, reflect the reigning atmosphere of political tension and confusion in Suriname during the time of Behn's visit in 1663 and 1664, though without assigning political labels to the disputants. In fact, the Lord Governor of Suriname to whom the novella refers is Francis, Lord Willoughby of Parham, an intimate of the royal family and of Lord Clarendon and a constant conspirator against the Protectorate, who had received his commission for settlements in Guiana and elsewhere in the Caribbean from Charles II, at his court in exile. Willoughby is absent during Behn's narrative, but the governor of the colony who orders Oroonoko's execution, William Byam, was a key figure in the Royalist struggle for control of Barbados in the previous decade, and likewise in Suriname battled continuously with the Parliamentarians in the colony. In 1662, immediately before Behn's arrival, Byam had accused a group of Independents, led by Robert Sandford, of conspiracy, and had summarily tried and expelled them from the colony. Sandford had owned the plantation neighboring that of Sir Robert Harley, St. John's Hill, which the narrator mentions as her residence. Harley also was a Royalist, and had been a friend of Willoughby, though a quarrel between

---

ert Harley from the Stewards of his Plantations in Suriname. 1663–1664";
V. T. Harlow's detailed introduction to this reprint collection, esp. xxvii–lv and lxvi–xcv; Goreau, *Reconstructing Aphra*, 66–69; Cyril Hamshere, *The British in the Caribbean* (Cambridge: Harvard University Press, 1972), 64–65; and James A. Williamson, *English Colonies in Guiana and on the Amazon, 1604–1668* (Oxford: Clarendon Press, 1923).

the two during Harley's chancellorship of Barbados had resulted in Willoughby's expulsion from that colony in 1664.
There were few firm friendships in the British Caribbean
in this tumultuous period of colonial adventurism. Indeed
in 1665, shortly after Behn left Suriname, Willoughby himself, in a visit to Guiana meant to restore orderly government to the colony, was nearly assassinated by John Allen,
who resented his recent prosecution for blasphemy and du-
eling.

Behn herself may have been engaged with these volatile
politics through an alliance with a radical named William
Scot, who went to the colony to escape prosecution for high
treason in England, and whose father Thomas was a prominent figure on the Parliamentary side in the revolution
and during the Commonwealth (Goreau, *Reconstructing
Aphra*, 66–69). The radical connection makes some sense in
that Byam, the notoriously ardent and high-handed Royalist, is clearly the villain of the piece, and Colonel George
Martin, Parliamentarian and brother to "*Harry Martin* the
great *Oliverian*" (*Oroonoko* 50), deplores the inhumanity of
Oroonoko's execution. But its relevance need not be directly personal. The first substantial antislavery statements
were voiced by the radical Puritans in the 1660s;[31] there was

31. Richard Baxter, *A Christian Directory, or, a Summ of Practical The-
ologie, and Cases of Conscience* (London, 1673), 557–60. Cited in Thomas E.
Drake, *Quakers and Slavery in America* (New Haven: Yale University Press,
1950), 3. Drake dates the section on slavery to 1664–65. Also sympathetic,
though less explicitly opposed to slavery, is George Fox, "To Friends Beyond the Sea That Have Blacks and Indian Slaves" (1657), in *A Collection
of Many Select and Christian Epistles, Letters and Testimonies* (London, 1698),
Epistle no. 153; cited in Drake, *Quakers and Slavery in America*, 5. On
Quakers, see also Davis, *The Problem of Slavery*, 304–26; Carl Bridenbaugh
and Roberta Bridenbaugh, *No Peace Beyond the Line: The English in the Caribbean, 1624–1690* (New York: Oxford University Press, 1972), 357–59;
and Herbert Aptheker, "The Quakers and Negro Slavery," *Journal of Negro History* 26 (1940): 331–62. An even earlier, unambiguous antislavery

a Quaker colony in Suriname during this period; and George
Fox visited the West Indies in 1671, where he urged the
inclusion of blacks at Friends' meetings.[32] Though as a
group the Quakers in the New World were ambivalent
about slave ownership, and often profited from the slave
trade themselves, individual Friends throughout this period enlarged upon Fox's early example. William Edmundson spoke against slavery in both the West Indies and New
England.[33] Planters in Barbados charged that Edmundson's
practice of holding meetings for blacks in Quaker homes
raised threats of rebellion, and in 1676 the colonial government passed a law to prevent "Quakers from bringing Negroes to their meetings" and allowing slaves to attend
Quaker schools.[34] Though most modern readers automatically assume that the early attack on slavery voiced in *Oroonoko* arose out of a spontaneous and natural humanitaria-
nism, the Puritan precedent enables us to see that Behn's
position did have an historical context and ground; in this
period such sentiments were potentially "natural" only to
specific groups.

But there is no simple political allegory available in
Behn's novella. Though the Royalist Byam is Oroonoko's
enemy, Behn describes Trefry, Oroonoko's friend, who was

---

statement from the radical Puritans appears in the Digger pamphlet *Ty-
ranipocrit Discovered* (1649), quoted in Christopher Hill, *The World Turned
Upside Down: Radical Ideas during the English Revolution* (Harmondsworth,
Middlesex: Penguin, 1975), 337.

32. See Drake, *Quakers and Slavery in America*, 6, for an account of Fox's
recorded sermons at this time. See also Bridenbaugh and Bridenbaugh,
No Peace Beyond the Line, 357.

33. Cited in Drake, *Quakers and Slavery in America*, 9–10: copy of a letter
by William Edmundson, dated at Newport, 19 July 1676, in Records of
New England Yearly Meeting, vol. 400, "Antient Epistles, Minutes and
Advices, or Discipline." See Drake for other examples of early Quaker
statements.

34. Cited in Drake, *Quakers and Slavery in America*, 8; see also Bridenbaugh and Bridenbaugh, *No Peace Beyond the Line*, 358.

in fact the overseer of Sir Robert Harley's plantation at St. John's Hill, as an agent of Willoughby's: Trefry must have been a Royalist. His open struggle with Byam over Oroonoko's fate might allude to divisions within the Royalist camp, divisions which were frequent and intense in Barbados, for instance, when Willoughby came to power in that colony. More important than direct political correspondences, however, is the tenor of political experience in the West Indies and Guiana in this period. For Behn and others, the colonies seemed to stage an anachronism, the repetition of the English revolution, and the political endpoint of Behn's narrative is nothing less than the reenactment of the most traumatic event of the revolution, the execution of Charles I.

From almost the instant of his beheading, the king's last days, and the climactic drama of his execution, were recounted by Royalist writers in a language that quickly established the discourse of Charles's suffering as heroic tragedy. *The Life of Charles I*, written just after the Restoration and close to the year in which Oroonoko's story is set, suggests the tenor of this discourse:

> He entred this ignominious and gastly Theatre with the same mind as He used to carry to His Throne, shewing no fear of death. . . . [Bloody trophies from the execution were distributed among the King's murderers at the execution and immediately thereafter]; some out of a brutish malice would have them as spoiles and trophees of their hatred to their Lawfull Sovereign. . . . He that had nothing Common in His Life and Fortune is almost profaned by a Vulgar pen. The attempt, I confess, admits no Apology but this, That it was fit that Posterity, when they read His Works . . . should also be told that His Actions were as Heroick as His Writings . . . Which not being undertaken by some Noble hand . . . I was by Importunity prevailed upon to imitate those affectionate Slaves, who would gather up the scattered limbs of some

great Person that had been their Lord, yet fell at the pleasure of his Enemies.[35]

Related images appear in a version published in 1681, shortly before the writing of *Oroonoko:*

> These Barbarous Regicides . . . his Bloody Murtherers . . . built a Scaffold for his Murther, before the Great Gate at *White Hall,* whereunto they fixed several Staples of Iron, and prepared Cords, to tye him down to the Block, had he made any resistance to that Cruel and Bloody stroke. . . . And then, most Christianly forgiving all, praying for his Enemies, he meekly submitted to the stroke of the Axe . . . he suffered as an Heroick Champion . . . by his patient enduring the many insolent affronts of this subtile, false, cruel, and most implacable Generation, in their Barbarous manner of conventing, and Condemning him to Death; and to see his most bloodthirsty Enemies then Triumph over him. . . . they have made him *Glorious* in his Memory, throughout the World, by a Great, Universal and most durable Fame.[36]

Charles I was evidently a powerful presence for Behn at the writing of *Oroonoko,* even though the story was composed only shortly before its publication in 1688, long after Charles's death, the Restoration, and even the intervening death of Charles II—the monarch with whom Behn's acquaintance and allegiance were much more immediate and personal. Oroonoko's heroism is attached to that of Charles I not just generically—in the affinity of "Great Men" of "mighty Actions" and "large Souls" (7, 47), which has linked all heroes in the epic tradition from Achilles to Anthony—but directly. Behn's slave-name for Oroonoko, Cae-

35. Richard Perrinchiefe, *The Life of Charles I,* in *The Workers of King Charles The Martyr* (London, 1662), 92–93, 118.
36. William Dugdale, *A Short View of the Late Troubles in England* (Oxford, 1681), 371–75.

sar, is the name she repeatedly used for the Stuart monarchs: Charles II is Caesar in her poem "A Farewell to Celladon on His Going Into Ireland" (1684) as is James II in her "Poem to Her Sacred Majesty Queen Mary" (1689) (Spengemann, "Earliest American Novel," 401). And Oroonoko's character, as we have already seen, is defined by his sympathy for Charles: "He had heard of the late Civil Wars in *England*, and the deplorable Death of our great Monarch; and wou'd discourse of it with all the Sense and Abhorrence of the Injustice imaginable" (*Oroonoko* 7). Sentenced, like Charles in these Royalist accounts, by the decree of a Council of "notorious Villains" (69) and irreverent swearers, and murdered by Banister, a "Fellow of absolute Barbarity, and fit to execute any Villainy" (76), "this great Man" (78), another royal martyr, endures his death patiently, "without a Groan, or a Reproach" (77). Even the narrator's final apology, though it refers specifically to female authorship, reproduces the conventional humble stance of the chroniclers of the king's death: "Thus died this great Man, worthy of a better Fate, and a more sublime Wit than mine to write his Praise; Yet, I hope, the Reputation of my pen is considerable enough to make his glorious Name to survive to all Ages" (78). "The Spectacle . . . of a mangled King" (77), then, with which we are finally presented at the close of the narrative,[37] when Oroonoko is

37. I am indebted to Adela Pinch for this reading of these lines. Paul J. Korshin describes Oroonoko's death as an instance of christomimetic martyrology (*Typologies in England 1650–1820* [Princeton: Princeton University Press, 1982], 213), a typology equally applicable to these accounts of Charles I's martyrdom; in this sense, these two martyrs could also be connected as types of Christ. George Guffey sees Oroonoko as a figure for James II ("Aphra Behn's *Oroonoko*: Occasion and Accomplishment," in *Two English Novelists: Aphra Behn and Anthony Trollope* [Los Angeles: William Andrews Clark Memorial Library, University of California, 1975]), an argument that Katharine M. Rogers finds "remarkably far-fetched" ("Fact and Fiction in Aphra Behn's *Oroonoko*," *Studies in the Novel* 20 [1988]: esp.

quartered and his remains are distributed around the colony, evokes with surprising vividness the tragic drama of Charles Stuart's violent death. The sense of momentous loss that Behn's narrative generates on behalf of the "royal slave" is the product of the hidden figuration in Oroonoko's death of the culminating moment of the English revolution.

But the tragedy is double in a larger sense. Abstractly, both Charles I and Oroonoko are victims of the same historical phenomenon—those new forces in English society loosely associated with an anti-absolutist mercantile imperialism. In England the rapid rise of colonization and mercantile trade coincided with the defeat of absolutism in the seventeenth century. Thus in a mediated sense the death of Charles I makes that of Oroonoko possible, and Oroonoko's death stands as a reminder of the massive historical shift that destroyed Charles Stuart and made England into a modern imperialist power. Ironically, in this context, both King Charles and the African slave in the new world are victims of the same historical force.

At this point we might imagine that the account of Oroonoko's death represents the moment of greatest mystification in the narrative, the proof of an absolute alterity in the confrontation between the colonialist and the native "other." What could be more divergent than the fate of Charles Stuart and that of an African slave? But in fact the violent yoking of these two figures provides the occasion for the most brutal and visceral contact that Behn's narrative makes with the historical experience of slavery in the West Indies and Guiana. Merely the information that Oro-

10 and n. 46). Rogers's main contention against Guffey is that Behn's treatment of slavery must be seen as a "serious concern," rather than presuming that the issue for Behn is simply subsumed by a Royalist allegory. Both sides of this debate, the typological and the serious, support my argument here.

onoko is a Koromantyn (*Oroonoko* 5) connects his story to contemporary historical testimony on slavery and rebellion in the colonies. Bryan Edwards describes the character of slaves from this area:

> The circumstances which distinguish the Koromantyn, or Gold Coast, Negroes, from all others, are firmness both of body and mind; a ferociousness of disposition; but withal, activity, courage, and a stubbornness, or what an ancient Roman would have deemed an elevation, of soul, which prompts them to enterprizes of difficulty and danger; and enables them to meet death, in its most horrible shape, with fortitude or indifference. . . . It is not wonderful that such men should endeavour, even by means the most desperate, to regain the freedom of which they have been deprived; nor do I conceive that any further circumstances are necessary to prompt them to action, than that of being sold into captivity in a distant country.[38]

Edwards is obviously also drawn to an epic romanticization, but his historical account begins to give us a conviction of

38. Bryan Edwards, *The History, Civil and Commercial, of the British Colonies in the West Indies*, 2 vols. (Dublin, 1793; reprint, New York: Arno Press, 1972), 2:59. Most of the detailed accounts of slavery in the West Indies and Guiana date from the later eighteenth century, but there is ample evidence of marronage, rebellion, and judicial torture throughout the West Indies and including Suriname from Behn's period on. Suriname passed out of British hands in 1667, and thus the fullest documentation of the treatment of rebel slaves in that country describes conditions under the Dutch. There is every reason to believe, however, in a continuity from British to Dutch practices historically in Suriname, just as there is every evidence of the same continuity throughout the West Indies and Guiana—British or Dutch—at any given moment in the long century and a half of active slave trade. For further documentation, in addition to the works cited in subsequent notes, see George Warren, *An Impartial Description of Surinam upon the Continent of Guiana in America* (London, 1667); *Historical Essay on the Colony of Suriname*, 1788, tr. Simon Cohen, ed. Jacob R. Marcus and Stanley F. Chyet (New York: Ktav Publishing House, 1974); Price, *Guiana Maroons*; and Price, ed., *Maroon Societies*.

the experience behind the romance in Behn's narrative. So common was rebellion among the Koromantyns, that the importation of slaves from the Gold Coast was stopped by the late eighteenth century to reduce the risk of insurrection.

Edwards goes on to recount one such rebellion in Jamaica in 1760, which "arose at the instigation of a Koromantyn Negro of the name of Tacky, who had been a chief in Guiney" (*History* 2: 59–60). He details in particular the execution of the rebel leaders, who were killed, like Oroonoko, to make "an Example to all the Negroes, to fright 'em from daring to threaten their Betters" (*Oroonoko* 70):

> The wretch that was burned was made to sit on the ground, and his body being chained to an iron stake, the fire was applied to his feet. He uttered not a groan, and saw his legs reduced to ashes with the utmost firmness and composure; after which one of his arms by some means getting loose, he snatched a brand from the fire that was consuming him, and flung it in the face of the executioner. (*History* 2: 61)

A correspondent from Jamaica to the *London Magazine* in 1767 provides a similar account: "Such of them [rebel Negroes] as fell into our hands, were burnt alive on a slow fire, beginning at their feet, and burning upwards. It would have surprized you to see with what resolution and firmness they bore the torture, smiling with an air of disdain at their executioners, and those about them."[39] And John Stedman, the period's most detailed reporter of the executions of rebel maroons, recounts the request of a man who had been broken on the rack: "I imagined him dead, and felt happy; till the magistrates stirring to depart, he writhed himself from the cross . . . rested his head on part

---

39. *London Magazine* 36 (May 1767), 94. Also cited in Davis, *The Problem of Slavery*, 477.

of the timber, and asked the by-standers for a pipe of tobacco."[40]

In the context of these firsthand accounts, Oroonoko's death takes on a significance entirely different from that conferred upon it through the paradigm of heroic romance or the figuration of the death of King Charles:

> [He] assur'd them, they need not tie him, for he would stand fix'd like a Rock, and endure Death so as should encourage them to die. . . . He had learn'd to take Tobacco; and when he was assur'd he should die, he desir'd they should give him a Pipe in his Mouth, ready lighted; which they did: And the executioner came, and first cut off his Members, and threw them into the Fire; after that, with an ill-favour'd Knife, they cut off his Ears and his Nose, and burn'd them; he still smoak'd on, as if nothing had touch'd him; then they hack'd off one of his Arms, and still he bore up, and held his Pipe; but at the cutting off the other Arm, his Head sunk, and his Pipe dropt and he gave up the Ghost, without a Groan, or a Reproach. (77)

As far as this horrible fictional scene takes us from the image of Dryden's Anthony or that of Charles Stuart, those radically irrelevant figures are the means by which this narrative finds its way to the historical experience of the Koromantyn slave—the means by which this passage offers not merely a fascination with the brutality that is depicted here and in the other historical materials I have cited, but a sym-

---

40. John Stedman, *Narrative of a Five Years' Expedition Against the Revolted Negroes of Surinam* (1796; reprint, Amherst: University of Massachusetts Press, 1972), 382. Stedman's book contains the fullest account available in this period of the punishments for maroons in the West Indies and Guiana. Price finds Stedman's descriptions "to have a solid grounding in fact," and he also shows that Suriname was the most brutal of the major plantation colonies of the New World (*Guiana Maroons*, 25, 9).

pathetic memorialization of those human beings whose sufferings these words recall.

In *Oroonoko* the superimposition of two modes of mystification—romantic and imperialist—crucially conjoined by the figure of the woman, produces an historical insight and a critical sympathy that the argument from alterity cannot explain. This is not to say that Behn herself is any more effective or unambivalent an emancipationist than we had originally suspected. But it does suggest that even though Behn's relationship with the colonial "other" is primarily a specular one—even though Behn can only see colonialism in the mirror of her own culture—that occluded vision has a potential critical dimension. As the familiar, "normalizing" figures of alterity, the romantic hero and his orderly codes of love, honor, and patient sacrifice, open up the experience of the "other," we can glimpse, in the contradictions of colonialist ideology, the workings of a radical contemporaneity.

I have tried to exemplify the notion of radical contemporaneity variously in this reading of Behn's novella. In Charles Stuart and Oroonoko we have seen two beings who could never meet in this world joined as historical contemporaries through the contradictory logic of Behn's imperialist romance. We have used a feminist reading of colonialist ideology, which places women at the center of the structures of rationalization that justify mercantile expansion, to ground an account of the formal and ideological contradictions surrounding the representation of race and slavery in this work. And concurrently we have juxtaposed the figure of the woman, ideological implement of a colonialist culture, with the figure of the slave, economic implement of the same system. Though Behn never clearly sees herself in the place of the African slave, the mediation of the figure of the woman between the two contradictory paradigms upon which her narrative depends uncovers a mutuality beyond her immediate awareness or control.

All of these relationships of contemporaneity spring from the failures of coherence in the discourse of *Oroonoko*, from the mutual interaction of the contradictory aristo-cratic and bourgeois paradigms that conjointly shape the novella. This interaction—contingent, temporary, and me-diatory—is the dialectical process that my reading of *Oro-onoko* has aimed to define, the process by which we may imagine Behn's text to "meet the Other on the same ground, in the same Time." By this means, we can position the African slave in Behn's novella not as a projection of colonialist discourse, contained or incorporated by a domi-nant power, but as an historical force in his own right and his own body. The notion of a relatively autonomous native position, of a site of resistance that is not produced and controlled by the ideological apparatuses of colonialist power, seems to me to have crucial consequences for our conclusions about colonialist ideology and for the implica-tions of a critique of imperialism or of ideology critique in general. It suggests that we can read the literature of those in power not only for the massive and elaborate means by which power is exercised, but also as a source of leverage for those in opposition, that although sites of resistance may be produced within a dominant ideology, they are not produced by it, and they do not serve it. They are pro-duced despite it, and they serve to locate opposition in a body and a language that even the colonialist can be made to understand.

3

Staging Sexuality:
Violence and Pleasure
in the Domestic She-Tragedy

> *Enter* Teramainta *wounded.*
> *Titus.*   Ha! My Teraminta!
> Is't possible? The very top of beauty,
> This perfect face drawn by the gods at council,
> Which they were long a-making, as they had reason,
> For they shall never hit the like again,
> Defiled and mangled thus! . . .
> *Teraminta.* . . . let me fall again among the people,
> Let me be hooted like a common strumpet,
> Tossed, as I was, and dragged about the streets,
> . . . .
> Thus to the goal of death, this happy end
> Of all my miseries, here to pant my last,
> To wash thy gashes with my farewell tears,
> To murmur, sob, and lean my aching head
> Upon thy breast, thus like a cradle babe
> To suck thy wounds and bubble out my soul.
> Nathaniel Lee, *Lucius Junius Brutus*

In 1714 Nicholas Rowe took public credit for the creation of a new dramatic mode, which he named for the gender of its protagonist. Rowe predicted, only half-ironically, that his already well-acclaimed "she-tragedies" would "o'errun the nation," if the trend toward moralized drama should continue.[1] Rowe's claim to have invented the she-tragedy, though largely justified by his role in its populariz-ation, has helped to obscure the significance of the tragic female protagonist both in the development of the drama and in the process of ideology formation by which the eco-nomic and social forces of mercantile capitalism were ac-commodated by and furthered in the literary culture of the period. Though Rowe named this new type of English trag-edy, he was neither its first, nor even its first successful, practitioner. During the last quarter of the seventeenth century, well before the beginning of Rowe's career, women acquired an unprecedented prominence in the drama. Many of the most celebrated and influential plays, includ-ing those of Thomas Otway, Nathaniel Lee, John Banks, and Thomas Southerne, depend specifically upon the des-ignation of a female protagonist. Earlier tragedy, of course, does not exclude women. Marlowe's drama is charac-teristically masculine, but Shakespeare's Cleopatra displays the force of a character conceived as strongly female. And though Cleopatra may be a comparative anomaly in Shake-speare's tragic corpus, the Jacobean dramatists turned con-sistently to women.

The she-tragedy of the late Restoration, however, is a unique instance of this focus on the representation of women. It portrays a new kind of heroine, whose victimiza-tion provides the essential material of the plot and whose defenselessness specifically contrasts with the defiance of the passionate and ambitious female characters in the pre-ceding heroic play. But more important, the rise of the she-tragedy seems to mark a meeting point of a series of promi-nent discursive shifts: an intense affective engagement with female suffering; a corollary and explicit interest in the fe-

1. Nicholas Rowe, *The Tragedy of Jane Shore*, ed. Harry William Ped-icord (London: Edward Arnold, 1975), Epilogue, line 29.

male body and female sexuality; a major change in the representation of class distinctions, including a transition toward the moralized and bourgeois forms of the mid-eighteenth century; and—in the case of Rowe—a striking and symptomatic leap from suffering female sexuality to commodification. The defenseless woman of this distinctive dramatic form is thus a figure that fuses a variety of ideological concerns, from domestic virtue and female passivity to rape, social chaos, and fetishization. Examining this figure can help us define the construction of female sexuality in this period, and expose the connection between this constitution of female sexuality and the process of commodification—a connection that will be the central concern of Chapter 4. Political critics, even when they focus on gender, have been slow to raise issues of sexuality; a reading of this drama might serve to demonstrate why the gap between the sexual and the sociopolitical has loomed so large. Indeed, a reading of the she-tragedy can help to bridge that gap by providing an example of the elusive articulation of sexuality, economics, and commodification.

The "she-tragedy" stands historically between the aristocratic heroic drama of the coterie Restoration theater and the "bourgeois tragedy" of Aaron Hill, George Lillo, Charles Johnson, or Edward Moore.[2] Beginning in the late 1670s, the major original serious drama of the English theater takes on a discernibly different shape from the programmatic love-and-honor conflicts that dominated the stage during the previous decade: it prefers pity to admiration and passive virtue to heroic self-assertion, and it turns consistently to private citizens, domestic material, and female protagonists. The early works in this pathetic or affec-

2. See my *English Dramatic Form, 1660–1760: An Essay in Generic History* (New Haven: Yale University Press, 1981).

tive mode retain the trappings of the heroic: Nathaniel Lee's *Rival Queens* (March 1677) and Dryden's *All for Love* (December 1677) both present the typical legendary and exotic characters of heroic drama. They treat those male protagonists, however, not as active heroes but as passive victims whose dramatic significance is defined by their pathetic situation rather than their aristocratic status. Symptomatically, the pathos of that situation is in both plays augmented by the sufferings of a weak and innocent female victim, who shares with the male protagonist the task of generating and sustaining the affective intensity of the drama. Dryden's Cleopatra is no queenly courtesan, but a "wife, a silly, harmless, household dove, / Fond without art, and kind without deceit."[3] The pitying response that she elicits defines her function in the plot and ultimately the significance of her and Antony's fate.

Thomas Otway's major serious plays of the early 1680s, however, provide the earliest and most powerful staging of the ideological problematic over which the pathetic female protagonist presides.[4] In *The Orphan* (1680) and *Venice Preserved* (1682) Otway essentially eliminates the representation of social status, even as a nominal label attached to a primarily pitiable character or as a nostalgic reflection of past heroism. In *Venice Preserved* his protagonist is a private citizen, in *The Orphan* an unattached and unclaimed woman. Though Jaffeir in the former play seems to have joined the struggle over the fate of the Venetian republic, his role is systematically anti-heroic: Venice serves as a formal prop to instigate and sustain his private, sexual crisis. And of

3. John Dryden, *All for Love*, ed. David M. Vieth (Lincoln: University of Nebraska Press, 1972), IV.92–93.
4. For a full and suggestive analysis of the affective mode, though from an ahistorical perspective, see Eric Rothstein, *Restoration Tragedy: Form and the Process of Change* (Madison: University of Wisconsin Press, 1967), esp. 126–27.

course *The Orphan*'s Monimia is by definition a figure of exclusively domestic concern. These characters are essentially passive and static; and though the powerlessness and victimization typical of Otway's major tragedy can be accommodated to a passive male protagonist such as Jaffeir, such qualities seem to be most easily and automatically represented in a woman.

Monimia is perhaps the most influential defenseless woman of the age. *The Orphan* remained in the repertory for almost two centuries, and Monimia is named as the inspiration or precursor of a series of sentimental plays from *The Ambitious Step-Mother* to *The London Merchant*: her effect is evident on the representation of suffering women throughout the period.[5] Indeed, Monimia's dilemma is a model for the eighteenth-century cult of sensibility, both formally and thematically. This form of influence suggests the cultural vitality of the feminization of dramatic tragedy. An account of the diverse and contradictory functions that Monimia performs in the structure of Otway's prominent she-tragedy will help to explain the special significance and utility of the passive female protagonist in the ideological formation of this period.

The Orphan's plot is simple and programmatic. Monimia, the orphan, falls in love with and secretly marries Castalio, the son of her guardian. His libertine twin brother, Polydore, interprets the lovers' plans for a secret consummation of their marriage as an illicit tryst, and takes Castalio's place in Monimia's bed. Thus the innocent Monimia is made to commit a kind of adultery, which brings down the whole idealized domestic male world of the play in an apocalyptic

5. For an account of the contemporary prominence of *The Orphan* on the stage, see Aline Mackenzie Taylor, *Next to Shakespeare: Otway's "Venice Preserv'd" and "The Orphan" and Their History on the London Stage* (Durham, N.C.: Duke University Press, 1950).

scene of death, suicide, and despair. Monimia takes poison; Polydore runs on Castalio's sword; and Castalio stabs himself. Thus Monimia's violation produces not one but three innocent victims, who fill the last two acts of the play with intertwined and overlapping curses and misunderstandings.

Monimia is a complex character, though not in the realist sense. She is first of all—for the purposes of the plot and of the audience's ongoing sympathy—"dove-like, soft, and kind,"[6] tender, weak, and innocent, despite the fact of her adultery, which is carefully staged to leave no suspicion of complicity on her part. Even as she kills herself in the final scene, she is described by Polydore as "innocent," "the trembling, tender, kind, deceived Monimia" (V.443 and 453). But this "dove-like" tenderness is also the basis of an evocation of female sexuality and in particular of the sexualized female body:

> *Castalio.*   Oh, thou art tender all!
> Gentle and kind as sympathizing Nature!
> When a sad story has been told, I've seen
> Thy little breasts, with soft compassion swelled,
> Shove up and down and heave like dying birds.
>   (III.273–77)

These birds seem to embody themselves out of the "dove-like" tenderness of the female figure. They epitomize her "sympathizing Nature" at the same time that they stand for her sexualized body, for those strangely disembodied or dismembered breasts are evoked consistently elsewhere in explicit connection with Monimia's sexuality, as when Polydore recalls sleeping with her:

6. Thomas Otway, *The Orphan,* ed. Aline Mackenzie Taylor (Lincoln: University of Nebraska Press, 1976), II.366.

> I'd trust thee with my life on those soft breasts!
> Breathe out the choicest secrets of my heart
> Till I had nothing in it left but love.
>
> (IV.390–92)

But the reembodiment of Monimia's breasts as dying birds, little prototypical victims themselves, represents a perverse conjunction of dismemberment, violence, and the female body that begins to suggest the nature of the play's treatment of female sexuality. Monimia's page, Cordelio, serves two functions—one, to keep Castalio occupied when Polydore takes his place in Monimia's bed; the other, to express the powerful image of simultaneous sexuality and violence that the "dying birds" condense. First, he sees Monimia in her bed, where her breasts take the place of a representation of her body:

> Madam, indeed I'd serve you with my soul;
> But in a morning when you call me to you,
> As by your bed I stand and tell you stories,
> I am ashamed to see your swelling breasts;
> It makes me blush, they are so very white.
>
> (I.220–24)

Then to Castalio the page repeats the account of Monimia "as she lay a-bed" (III.485), only this time with the addition of the violence that is so concisely indicated in the image of the "dying birds":

Yes, and I sung her the story you made too. And she did so sigh and so look with her eyes; and her breasts did so lift up and down. I could have found in my heart to have beat 'em, for they made me ashamed. (III.487–90)

Here the "birds" are being figuratively "beaten" in the course of the observer's sexual arousal. This violence finds an even more direct expression in Monimia's own figure for her plight as a result of Castalio's anger:

> Cruel as tigers o'er their trembling prey.
> I feel him in my breast, he tears my heart,
> And at each sigh he drinks the gushing blood.
> Must I be long in pain?
>
> (IV.156–60)

Violence and pain are prominent categories in this play. The female victim's pain is the obvious objective of the plot. But pain is connected not only with female sexuality, but, perversely and masochistically, with "pleasure" as well. Monimia in a conciliatory gesture appeals to Castalio to "lean / Upon my breasts and tell me where's thy pain" (IV.104–6), and Castalio finds pain and pleasure inseparable in his account of his desire for Monimia:

> No creeping slave, though tractable and dull
> As artful woman for her ends would choose,
> Shall ever dote as I have done; for, oh,
> No tongue my pleasure nor my pain can tell:
> 'Tis Heav'n to have thee, and without thee Hell.
>
> (II.387–91)

Polydore similarly joins pain and pleasure, sexuality and violence, in his fantasy of raping Monimia:

> It shall be so. I'll yet possess my love,
> Wait on, and watch her loose unguarded hours;
> Then, when her roving thoughts have been abroad
> And brought in wanton wishes to her heart—
> I'th' very minute when her virtue nods,

> I'll rush upon her in a storm of love,
> Bear down her guard of honor all before me,
> Surfeit on joys till even desire grows sick:
> Then by long absence, liberty regain
> And quite forget the pleasure and the pain.
>
> (I.367–78)

As we have seen, Monimia's own tenderness is defined by
the same conjunction of pleasure and pain—the "compassion" she feels at a "sad story." The "sad story" and Monimia's prototypical response to it stand for the audience's
pleasurably sympathetic response to Monimia's own pain
and thus epitomize the play's affective aesthetic. The passive female protagonist of this play, then, serves to define
the nature of female sexuality by calling up a fragmented
and ultimately violated image of the female body. This violence not only forms the substance of the plot, but also in
its implication with pleasure constitutes the play's affect:
the aesthetic pleasure at which the play aims, like the sexual
pleasure attributed to the rapist or the perverse pleasure
recounted by the injured lover, results from the pain in-
flicted upon the innocent woman or the sadomasochistic
enjoyment of self-inflicted pain.

The brutality with which the female protagonist is punished and the formal satisfaction or "pleasure" that violence
ultimately purveys do not follow from the surface assertions of her passivity and sexual inexperience. Indeed, in
retrospect, that unclaimed and helpless female figure is
structurally the instrument of apocalypse, the instrument
through which the microcosmic patriarchal ideal of the
play is destroyed. That is, in the logic of the narrative, the
purportedly passive female protagonist wields a cataclysmic
power well beyond the reach or even the ambition of any of
the male characters, a threat that does more to explain the
cruelty of her punishment than do any superficial accounts

of her innocence or passivity. Significantly, female power is prominently thematized in the metaphorical discourse of the play. When Castalio briefly relents toward Monimia, his desire for her is represented as her control over him and rendered in terms of emasculation by the sexualized female body:

> I cannot hear Monimia's soul's in sadness,
> And be a man. . . .
> Oh, I will throw m'impatient arms about her;
> In her soft bosom sigh my soul to peace,
> Till through the panting breast she finds the way
> To mould my heart, and make it what she will.
>
> (V.187–94)

Female power is also evoked in conventional metaphorical descriptions of women as tyrants (V.226) and men as their slaves (IV.122, V.281). These typical tropes of contemporary misogynist poetry indicate anxieties about female autonomy, sexual energy, and the social leveling produced by the resulting promiscuity. The passive protagonist thus takes on a threatening activity that is outside the play's explicit account of her character. Similarly, her status as an unattached orphan dissolves in the course of the plot into an ominous multiplicity of relationships, in which her sexuality pits all the men in her vicinity against each other. Monimia's multiple connections represent another indirect evocation of female power, the power to intercede between men, to break the bonds of patriarchy, and to disrupt stable male relationships and hierarchies. Monimia is not by this means endowed with power or with status as a character. Rather, her asserted passivity and her lack of status contradict the power and the multiple connections that attach to her in the process of the plot. Her sexuality is constituted by the violence directed at her passivity, and that violence is itself a response to the structural threat of her sexuality as it acts upon the male characters in her domestic realm. Thus female sexuality is both discursively passive and structurally threatening, an object of violence both on account of its vulnerability and on account of its power; the violence that it programmatically elicits both constitutes it and is provoked by it, and its violation is both a source of pleasure and an assertion of vengeance. From this constellation of contradictions we can begin to infer the nature of the female figure in the she-tragedy; a further look at this figure will help us to define its function in the dominant ideological structures of the period.

Under the general ideological rubric of misogyny and sadomasochism, the problematic perversity of Otway's play is equally evident in the works of the other major she-tragedians of this period, John Banks and Thomas Southerne.[7] The emotionalism and the self-consciously Shakespearean "naturalness" of their language establish a context of sympathetic immediacy for the dilemmas they depict. Their stories are typically shaped to produce and sustain a high level of physical or psychological violence. They resort frequently to scenes of madness, suicide, or sexual violation. And, most important, they rely consistently for the process of their plots and especially for their climactic crises upon offering some visible violence to the female victim—to characters such as Monimia, Belvidera (*Venice Preserved*), Anna Bullen (Banks, *Virtue Betrayed*, 1682), Erminia (Southerne, *The Disappointment*, 1684), Isabella (Southerne, *The Fatal Marriage*, 1694), or Imoinda (Southerne, *Oroonoko*, 1695).

7. In his "Restoration Tragedy: A Reconsideration," *Durham University Journal* 11 (June 1950): 106–15, Clifford Leech aptly describes the "strenuous emotional exercise" that this form entails.

In many of these plays, the representations of female sexuality follow very closely the model of Monimia. Southerne's *Fatal Marriage* tells in its primary tragic plot the heartrending tale of another accidental adultery. Isabella's husband Biron has been missing at sea for seven years, and in a state of penury and near starvation she marries her long-time suitor and benefactor Villeroy. Immediately after the consummation, Biron reappears, with the predictable results of death and suicide. This play, like Otway's, expresses the same sadomasochistic aesthetic of "pleasing pain,"[8] located in the same sexualized engagement with the suffering of the female victim. Isabella is an "out-cast Wretch," "Abandon'd . . . and lost," a "Bankrupt every way," and evidently "born to suffer" (I.iii.2; II.ii.16, 17; II.ii.66). Of herself, she accurately asserts that:

> the Unfortunate cannot be Friends:
> Fate watches the first motion of the Soul,
> To disappoint our wishes; if we pray
> For Blessings, they prove curses in the end,
> To ruin all about us.
>   (I.iii.9–13)

The plot of this play centers, of course, on Isabella's sexuality and its disturbing transferability. Biron is the first object of her "Pleasures" (II.iii.90); Villeroy is confident of his own abilities in that regard:

> O extasie of Joy!
> Leave that to me. If all my Services,
> If prosperous Days, and kind indulging Nights,

---

8. Thomas Southerne, *The Fatal Marriage; or, the Innocent Adultery*, I.iii.32, in vol. 1 of *The Works of Thomas Southerne*, ed. Robert Jordan and Harold Love, 2 vols. (Oxford: Clarendon Press, 1988). Subsequent references to this play are to this edition.

> If all that Man can fondly say, or do,
> Can beget Love, Love shall be born again.
> (II.iii.122–26)

And his prediction is apparently accurate, since he arises after their wedding night "in a rare good humor" (III.ii.143). Biron, when he returns, meets Isabella in her bedchamber, and though he is greeted by an enigmatic fit of hysterics, gets right to the point:

> Compose thy self, my Love!
> The fit is past; all may be well again.
> Let us to Bed.
> (IV.iii.237–40)

But at last instead of bed, Biron, bloody and fatally wounded, achieves his consummation with a "long farewell, and a last parting Kiss" (V.iv.43), and Isabella, "*distracted, held by her Women, her Hair dishevel'd*" (V.iv.251 *sd.*), stabs herself and dies in despair. These final, mortal consummations take the place of the sexual consummation that preoccupies these characters throughout the play and explicitly merge violence and female sexuality.

Rowe's she-tragedies thus mark the culmination of an established ideological and generic pattern. The defenseless woman had for three decades been a familiar and formally central figure upon the English stage, as Rowe himself, an able dramatic historian, was the first to admit. In the Dedication and Prologue of his apprentice work, *The Ambitious Step-Mother* (1700), Rowe evokes this precedent to define and defend his own practice:

> If Dying Lovers yet deserve a Tear,
> If a sad Story of a Maid's Despair
> Yet move Compassion in the pitying Fair,

> This Day the Poet does his Art employ,
> The soft Accesses of your Souls to try
> . . . .
> Nor let the Men, the weeping Fair accuse
> Those kind Protectors of the Tragick Muse,
> Whose Tears did moving *Otway*'s Labours crown,
> And made the poor *Monimia*'s Grief their own:
> Those Tears, their Art, not Weakness has confest,
> Their Grief approv'd the Niceness of their Tast,
> And they wept most, because they judg'd the best.[9]

Rowe's major she-tragedies, *The Fair Penitent* (1703), *Jane Shore* (1714), and *Lady Jane Gray* (1715), all bear a very close resemblance to the affective dramas of Otway, Banks, and Southerne. Rowe's heroines are beset and injured martyrs, whose plights and consequent sufferings make up the substance and aim of their plots. But, unlike their predecessors, Rowe's plays do not end in pure affect.

In *The Fair Penitent*, which depicts a domestic dilemma essentially identical to that of *The Orphan*, the titular female protagonist Calista is no unwitting victim, but an erring lover who trusts a false libertine, Lothario, but is forced into an arranged marriage with the admirable Altamont. The "fair penitent" of this play is thus made to take moral responsibility for the sexual transgression that *The Orphan* attributes to accident. Her repentant death supplies the tragedy with a lesson:

> By such examples are we taught to prove
> The sorrows that attend unlawful love;
> Death or some worse misfortunes soon divide
> The injured bridegroom from his guilty bride;

9. Nicholas Rowe, *The Ambitious Step-Mother*, 2d ed. (London: printed for R. Wellington and Thomas Osborne, 1702), sig. A4^r.

> If you would have the nuptial union last,
> Let virtue be the bond that ties it fast.[10]

Calista is sexually a version of Monimia, though her complicity and guilt initially contradict the prototypical pathetic
tenderness and innocence of the female victim. These are
affectively reserved for the last scenes of the play, when she
repents and dies. But even in the first act, though Calista is
described at one point as "haughty, insolent, / And fierce
with high disdain" (I.139–40) in order to confer some plau-
sibility upon her willing alliance with Lothario, the pull of
pathos largely contradicts this view. Lothario describes her
as "gentle, kind" (I.135), and his first encounter with her
reproduces all the familiar motifs of warmth, fondness, and
tender breasts:

> I found the fond, believing, love-sick maid
> Loose, unattired, warm, tender, full of wishes;
> Fierceness and pride, the guardians of her honor,
> Were charmed to rest, and love alone was waking.
> Within her rising bosom all was calm
> As peaceful seas that know no storms and only
> Are gently lifted up and down by tides.
> I snatched the glorious, golden opportunity,
> And with prevailing, youthful ardor pressed her,
> Till with short sighs and murmuring reluctance
> The yielding fair one gave me perfect happiness.
> Ev'n all the livelong night we passed in bliss,
> In ecstasies too fierce to last forever.
>
> (I.149–61)

It is significant that the thematization of tenderness and
softness in this play, as in *The Orphan*, entails a parallel fem-

10. Nicholas Rowe, *The Fair Penitent*, ed. Malcolm Goldstein (Lincoln:
University of Nebraska Press, 1969), V.288–93. Subsequent references to
this play will be to this edition.

inization of the admirable male protagonist. Here Altamont, in his love for Calista, himself is described in terms
typically applied to the suffering woman:

> Turn, and behold where gentle Altamont
> Kind as the softest virgin of our sex,
> And faithful as the simple village swain
> That never knew the courtly vice of changing,
> Sighs at your feet and woos you to be happy.
>
> (II.i.12–17)

Calista's sexuality, like Monimia's and Isabella's, comprises
the central problem of the plot. But in this case, Calista is
an explicit source of inscrutability; the men around her are
completely unable to determine from her external de-
meanor her engagement in "unlawful love." This sexual inscrutability produces her power in the action; through her
hypocrisy, she separates Altamont from his best friend:

> From thy false friendship to her arms I'll fly;
> There if in any pause of love I rest,
> Breathless with bliss, upon her panting breast,
> In broken, melting accents I will swear
> Henceforth to trust my heart with none but her;
> Then own the joys which on her charms attend
> Have more than paid me for my faithless friend.
>
> (III.350–56)

Monimia and Isabella, too, are sexually problematic; the
unresolved questions surrounding their sexual connections
produce the primary tensions of their plots. Here, however, the female body, with its familiar breasts, becomes an
explicit center of ambiguity and ironic tension, in a way
that we will find to be symptomatic of the sexualized female
figure later in the period.

Using the same situation, then, and preserving much of

the style, the material, and the effect of Otway's play, Rowe creates a penitential female victim with a significant sexual ambiguity and supplies her tale with moral tags that transform undiscriminating affect into didactic ethical assertion. That assertion, as we shall see, although it does not supersede the affective attractions of the suffering heroine, does play a role in the transition to a more explicitly bourgeois form.

Jane Shore provides another symptomatic account of the mixing of pleasure and pain, the superimposition of passivity and power, the equation of sexuality and violence, all in the name of the affective aesthetic of sensibility. But this play also enables us to see the connection between that affective aesthetic and the process of commodification that characterizes the representation of the female figure in the literary discourse of the period. *Jane Shore* recounts the tragic fate of Edward IV's mistress, who is carried off from the arms of a doting husband, seemingly almost against her will, by the dashing young king. The play is set years later, when, in the course of the political turmoil that follows the king's death, Jane is betrayed by her friend Alicia and Alicia's lover Hastings and eventually turned out into the streets, where she dies after a reunion and reconciliation with her loyal husband, negotiated by the compassionate Bellmour. Like Monimia, Jane Shore is "a poor, undone, forsaken, helpless woman," "sunk in grief, and pining with despair."[11] The pity elicited within the play and from the audience by her pain reflects her own prototypical compassionate response to suffering. She has performed "gentle deeds of mercy" among

11. Nicholas Rowe, *The Tragedy of Jane Shore*, III.i.52 and I.ii.69, in *British Dramatists from Dryden to Sheridan*, ed. George H. Nettleton and Arthur E. Case (Boston: Houghton Mifflin, 1939). Subsequent references will be to this edition.

the poor, the pris'ner,
The fatherless, the friendless, and the widow,
Who daily own the bounty of [her] hand.
(I.ii.171–73)

Like Monimia's, Jane Shore's suffering is sexualized and embodied, though here the female body is incarnated even more ambivalently in the disheveled "tresses" of the victim. Like Isabella, whose disheveled hair indicates the crisis in her suffering sexuality, Jane Shore is described at the height of her torture and distress in a stage direction: "*Enter* JANE SHORE, *her hair hanging loose on her shoulders, and barefooted*" (V.i.141 *sd*). In fact, hair is the successor to breasts in the sublimation of the representation of the body in this drama. Bellmour's use of this image concisely connects sexuality and suffering:

And on her shoulders, carelessly confused,
With loose neglect her lovely tresses hung.
Upon her cheek a faintish flush was spread;
Feeble she seemed, and sorely smit with pain,
While barefoot as she trod the flinty pavement,
Her footsteps all along were marked with blood.
(V.i.23–28)

This blood is anticipated by the tragic protagonist herself, in an ironic expression of gratitude to the would-be rapist Hastings shortly before he assaults her: "Mourning and bleeding for my past offences, / My fervent soul shall breathe one prayer for you" (II.i.164–67). Just after this speech, Jane Shore, like Monimia, undergoes the obligatory rape attempt, in which her body is held up, physically and discursively, for observation:

> Come, let me press thee, (*laying hold on her*)
> Pant on thy bosom, sink into thy arms,
> And lose myself in the luxurious fold.
>
> (II.i.222–24)

The scenes of Jane Shore's greatest misery accord with the most concrete representations of her sexualized body as well as with her reconciliation with her husband, who rushes to her side when he hears from Bellmour of those loosened tresses:

> If all her former woes were not enough,
> Look on her now; behold her where she wanders,
> Hunted to death, distressed on every side,
> With no one hand to help; and tell me, then,
> If ever misery were known like hers.
>
> (V.i.106–10)

This is a misery that again calls its own innocence and helplessness into question, and through the same conventional metaphors of tyranny and empire that we observed in *The Orphan*. In her years with Edward, Jane Shore has tasted a degree of female power to which the most ambitious might aspire. As her friend Alicia describes her status:

> What could we wish, we who delight in empire,
> Whose beauty is our sovereign good, and gives us
> Our reasons to rebel and power to reign—
> What could we more than to behold a monarch,
> Lovely, renowned, a conqueror, and young,
> Bound in our chains, and sighing at our feet?
>
> (I.ii.75–80)

Indeed, the play makes Alicia responsible for the most explicit assertions of threatening female power. Here she curses Hastings:

> . . . but know, proud lord,
> Howe'er thou scorn'st the weakness of my sex,
> This feeble hand may find the means to reach thee,
> How'er sublime in pow'r and greatness placed,
> With royal favor guarded round and graced;
> On eagle's wings my rage shall urge her flight,
> And hurl thee headlong from thy topmost height;
> Then like thy fate, superior will I sit,
> And view thee fall'n and grov'ling at my feet;
> See thy last breath with indignation go,
> And tread thee sinking to the shades below.
>   (II.i.121–32)

Alicia does cause Hastings's death, and Jane Shore causes the deaths of her husband and her only friend Bellmour, just as she and Alicia seem to act as agents in the contemporary political crisis surrounding the succession. In this sense, a major historical event, the execution of Hastings and eventual execution of the royal children, seems shaped and directed by female passion. Jane Shore is affectively innocent and theoretically powerless, but she is brutally punished for the threatening power that arises from her sexuality, and her subsequent suffering confirms that threat, as it epitomizes and embodies that sexuality.

Unlike Monimia, however, Jane Shore has another female identity, linked but not identical with her sexuality. At the crisis of her public violation, with her loosened tresses and bleeding feet, she undergoes a figurative conversion to commodification. Shore's desire for her is expressed, even at this moment when she is virtually undressed, in terms of the objects with which he would adorn her:

> Oh, that form!
> That angel-face on which my dotage hung!
> How I have gazed upon her, till my soul

With very eagerness went forth towards her,
And issued at my eyes. Was there a gem
Which the sun ripens in the Indian mine,
Or the rich bosom of the ocean yields,
What was there art could make, or wealth could buy,
Which I have left unsought to deck her beauty?

(V.i.73–81)

And he subsequently defines her very suffering by reference to the products of mercantile capitalism:

And can she bear it? Can that delicate frame
Endure the beating of a storm so rude?
Can she, for whom the various seasons changed
To court her appetite and crown her board,
For whom the foreign vintages were pressed,
For whom the merchant spread his silken stores,
Can she—
Intreat for bread, and want the needful raiment
To wrap her shivering bosom from the weather?

(V.i.111–19)

The ultimate emblem of their dying reconciliation is yet
another "costly" object of exchange, evoked this time by
Jane Shore:

I well remember
With what fond care, what diligence of love,
You lavished out your wealth to buy me pleasures,
Preventing every wish. Have you forgot
The costly string of pearl you brought me home
And tied about my neck?—How could I leave you?

(V.i.364–69)

Suddenly, at the climax of her suffering and her sexualiza-
tion, the female protagonist is represented in terms of
pearls, gems, and silks—contemporary tropes for the en-

terprises of mercantile capitalism. It is significant that she is most destitute, outcast, and entirely unadorned at the very point of her persistent figurative adornment with these products of trade. In this sense, commodification is offered as a natural and essential extension of female sexuality, and even of the female body itself. As we have seen, that body is constituted by the violence it elicits, and that violence is a discursive product of the construction of female sexuality as passive and vulnerable, a structural product of the implicit allusion to female power, and thus an ideological assertion of vengeance against the threat of the unruly woman.

As an extension of female sexuality, then, commodification also extends that constitutive passivity to the absolute emptiness of fetishization; that is, the stasis and the consequent lack of status of the female figure result in an emptying out of significance that coincides with the process by which fetishization empties bodies, beings, and practices of all significance except their exchangeability with objects. Furthermore, in this context commodification is propped upon the threat of female power: though commodification does not directly allude to female power, it emerges from an ideological paradigm based upon a fundamental anxiety about female sexual energy. And finally, in this constellation of contradictory propositions about female sexuality, commodification takes the place of violence against women; in other words, the figure of commodification is superimposed upon the brutal violation of the female body, and through that superimposition, comes to supersede it. The surprising integration of commodification into the discursive structures of this drama suggests that the ideological enterprise of commodification in general in the period might be usefully viewed in the light of violence, passivity, female sexuality and difference, and the contradictory threat of female power. When we turn in the next chapter to the theme of dressing in the aesthetic discourse of the early eighteenth century, we will have a fuller view of the complicated phenomenon of commodification and its connections with sexuality.

The constitution of female sexuality in the she-tragedy mediates or facilitates a process of female commodification, which in the first half of the eighteenth century becomes one of the dominant modes in the representation of women. From the perspective of the feminization of ideology, the she-tragedy thus has a distinctive mediatory function. Generically too, the she-tragedy mediates between an aristocratic and a bourgeois form.[12] These two processes of mediation, as we shall see, are themselves significantly connected. The works of George Lillo exemplify the bourgeois dimension of this affective drama. His plays join affect with morality, like Rowe's she-tragedies, but they take a step beyond moral assertion to construct a detailed ethics for the bourgeois protagonist. Lillo's major tragedies, *The London Merchant* (1731) and *Fatal Curiosity* (1736), both build toward emotional climaxes of mistake, misfortune, and death rivaling anything in Otway's or Southerne's she-tragedies. But Lillo's drama displays a strong internal ethical hierarchy by which every character's worth is carefully classified and against which every act is explicitly judged. Thorowgood of *The London Merchant* is a paragon of bourgeois morality, and his disquisitions on the merits of the merchant class establish the ethical assumptions of the play. Barnwell, his virtuous but tragically misled apprentice, is affectively innocent and defenseless, like Monimia, but technically and moralistically guilty, like Jane Shore, so that

---

12. For a more extensive account of my view of this transition and a fuller reading of the relevant plays, see my *English Dramatic Form.*

while his crimes can serve as the basis for the construction
of a system of bourgeois values, his sufferings can provide
the conventional pleasures of affective form. In this sense,
Barnwell stands in for the female protagonist of the she-
tragedy, and even the familiar problematic of sexuality—
with its passivity, its victimization, and its ambiguous evocation of a sexualized body—finds its way into his representation. In principle, Barnwell's ideal partner is apparently
Thorowgood's daughter Maria, who is in love with him
from the beginning of the play. But despite this potential
connection, and even despite Barnwell's affair with the
prostitute Millwood, his most affectively powerful relationship is with his friend and fellow apprentice Trueman, and
it is with Trueman that he conducts the conventionally sexualized crisis scene, complete with tears, compassion, victimization, breasts and bosoms, physical contact, imminent
death, and of course, pleasure and pain:

> *Trueman.* We have not yet embraced, and may be interrupted.
> Come to my arms!
> *Barnwell.* Never, never will I taste such joys on earth; never
> will I so soothe my just remorse. Are those honest arms and
> faithful bosom fit to embrace and to support a murderer? . . .
> (*Throwing himself on the ground.*) . . .
> *Trueman.* . . . Thy miseries cannot lay thee so low but love will
> find thee. (*Lies down by him.*) . . . Our mutual groans shall echo
> to each other through the dreary vault. Our sighs shall num-
> ber the moments as they pass, and mingling tears communi-
> cate such anguish as words were never made to express.
> *Barnwell.* Then be it so! [*Rising.*] Since you propose an inter-
> course of woe, pour all your griefs into my breast, and in
> exchange take mine. (*Embracing.*) Where's now the anguish
> that you promised? You've taken mine and make me no re-
> turn. Sure, peace and comfort dwell within these arms, and
> sorrow can't approach me while I'm here. This, too, is the

work of Heaven who, having before spoke peace and pardon
to me, now sends thee to confirm it. Oh, take, take some of
the joy that overflows my breast!

Trueman. I do, I do! Almighty Power, how have you made us
capable to bear, at once, the extremes of pleasure and of
pain.[13]

The implicit sexual connection between these two characters seems to arise primarily as a result of Barnwell's feminization; at this point and elsewhere in the play he takes
the position that we have typically seen occupied by a
woman, and concurrently the seducer Millwood takes the
position typically assigned to a man. Thus Millwood's sexuality is almost entirely neglected, whereas Barnwell's is a
product of his victimization and his passivity; it is intimately
tied to his pathetic death; and it gives rise to that perverse
affective connection of pleasure and pain that joins violence with vengeance in the she-tragedy. Here, however,
the suffering protagonist is also an object lesson in the in-
culcation of bourgeois virtue, and pleasure and pain are
moralistically superimposed upon an allusion to the repen-
tance trope of Puritan autobiography.

Thus, in *The London Merchant*, as well as in Lillo's *Fatal
Curiosity*, Aaron Hill's *Fatal Extravagance* (1721), or Edward
Moore's *Gamester* (1735), the suffering woman is replaced
by the middle-class male hero. Lillo's explicit ambition is to
create a moral tragedy with a private citizen as its protagonist, to produce a drama for a bourgeois audience whose
universal identification with the story will effect a universal
moral reformation in the populace. These aims are expressed explicitly in his dedication to *The London Merchant*:
"Tragedy is so far from losing its dignity by being accom-

13. George Lillo, *The London Merchant*, ed. William H. McBurney (Lincoln: University of Nebraska Press, 1965), V.v.29–56. Subsequent references will be to this edition.

modated to the circumstances of the generality of mankind
that it is more truly august in proportion to the extent of its
influence and the numbers that are properly affected by it"
(3). Unlike the heroic drama, then, this bourgeois tragedy
presumes to speak directly for its audience in a style designed to disguise the distinction between art and everyday
life. It makes a direct association between the moral standards it applies to its characters and the sympathetic emotional response of its audience, and the audience is then
meant to enact those standards in the real world. This sympathy closely resembles in its affective appeal the compassion and pleasure essential to the she-tragedy's depiction of
female suffering, but bourgeois tragedy associates that affect with a specific doctrine.

Thus the she-tragedy places the figure of the woman in a
pivotal spot in the literary culture of the early eighteenth
century: women mediate a major generic transition, and at
the same time they facilitate a significant ideological process. These functions suggest that the representation of
women is a key factor in the ideological structures of the
literary culture of this period, that the female figure has a
unique appropriateness, a special vitality in the complex social and cultural conjunctures of the age. If we situate the
female protagonist of the she-tragedy in her historical context, setting the generic against the ideological transition,
the passive protagonist against the commodity, we can use
these two crucial functions to illuminate each other.

The female protagonist who plays these dual mediatory
roles reflects a major transformation in English society, just
as she facilitates the cultural consolidation of that transformation. This change can be variously described as demo-
graphic, political, commercial, ideological, social, and economic. Its origins can be traced to the revolutionary period,
to the sixteenth century, or even to the genesis of English

absolutism in the late fifteenth century. It was extensive, pervasive, and fundamental, and its ultimate effect was the creation of the modern British mercantile and imperialist nation state.

A particular stage of this transformation occurred in the century after 1650. Although significant interpretive debates about the nature and meaning of this stage of this transformation remain unresolved, recent historians concur in their judgment of its contours and chronology. Lawrence Stone has designated the period from the mid-seventeenth century to the end of the eighteenth century as one of profound change in familial structure and domestic relationships.[14] Christopher Hill sees in the last years of the "century of revolution" (1660–1714) the ultimate ascendancy of a new social and economic system based increasingly upon a money economy and capitalist production.[15] D. C. Coleman, while recognizing the continuity of the pre-industrial English economy, finds in the century from 1650 to 1750 a new economic context both representing and heralding "real change."[16] Neil McKendrick locates in the course of the eighteenth century the various and diffuse forces that bring about what he calls "the birth of a consumer society."[17] These scholars and others generally agree that the social and economic transformation well under way by the early eighteenth century entailed the rapid urbanization of the populace, the monetarization of the economy,

14. Lawrence Stone, *The Family, Sex and Marriage in England, 1500–1800* (New York: Harper & Row, 1977).

15. Christopher Hill, *The Century of Revolution, 1603–1714* (1961; reprint, New York: Norton, 1966), 193–311.

16. D. C. Coleman, *The Economy of England, 1450–1750* (London: Oxford University Press, 1977), esp. 91–110.

17. Neil McKendrick, "The Consumer Revolution of Eighteenth-Century England," in Neil McKendrick, John Brewer, and J. H. Plumb, *The Birth of a Consumer Society: The Commercialization of Eighteenth-Century England* (Bloomington: Indiana University Press, 1982), 9–33.

the "commercialization" of the society, and the growth of wage labor, and affected the organization of labor, the definition of class status, the nature of the marketplace, the structure of domestic relations, and the theories and ideals of female behavior.[18]

Although the household workshop remained the dominant productive center, at least until the Industrial Revolution, this period saw an increase both in large-scale manufacturing and in the employment of wage labor. Of particular importance was the long enclosure movement, which forced the consolidation of small holdings, the capitalization of farming, the increase in agricultural specialization, the consequent rural depopulation, dramatic changes in the nature of the market, an increased sexual division of labor, and the gradual undermining of the family economy.[19] Related to these developments in agriculture was the enormous growth of a class of prosperous tradesmen—shopkeepers and retailers who were no longer directly involved in manufacture.[20] One effect of this social change was a reduction in the economic value of urban middle-class women, who

18. See, for example, Barrington Moore, *Social Origins of Dictatorship and Democracy: Lord and Peasant in the Making of the Modern World* (Boston: Beacon, 1966), chap. 1; Maurice Ashley, *England in the Seventeenth Century*, rev. ed. (1960; reprint, Baltimore: Penguin Books, 1962), esp. 232–52; J. H. Plumb, *England in the Eighteenth Century* (1950; reprint, Baltimore: Penguin Books, 1974), esp. 11–27; P. Deane, "The Industrial Revolution and Economic Growth: The Evidence of Early British National Income Estimates," in *The Causes of the Industrial Revolution in England*, ed. R. M. Hartwell (London: Methuen, 1967), 81–96; and J. R. Jones, *Country and Court: England, 1658–1714* (Cambridge: Harvard University Press, 1978), esp. 71–94 and 357–60. For the opposing position, see Peter Laslett, *The World We Have Lost*, 2d ed. (London: Methuen, 1971), who considers the industrial revolution of the late eighteenth century to be the locus of the only important change in English history.

19. See Bridget Hill, *Women, Work, and Sexual Politics in Eighteenth-Century England* (Oxford: Basil Blackwell, 1989), 47–68.

20. W. A. Speck, *Stability and Strife: England, 1714–1760* (Cambridge: Harvard University Press, 1977), 50–51 and 297–98.

became consumers rather than producers for their families and the marketplace. At the same time, a wife gradually lost any connection with her husband's labor, and hence the ability to contribute to the business or to assume the trade after his death.[21]

Thus working-class women were forced to carry their household skills to the marketplace, and there to compete for the lowest and worst-paying wage-labor in the unprotected trades, and middle-class women were removed from the economy and consequently placed in a position of extreme economic dependence;[22] a husband became the only respectable means of support. The patriarchal legal system, by vesting title to all family property in the male

21. Alice Clark's *The Working Life of Women in the Seventeenth Century* (London: George Routledge, 1919) covers the earlier part of this period; Bridget Hill's *Women, Work, and Sexual Politics in Eighteenth-Century England*, the latter. See especially Clark, 196, and Hill, 48–51. See also Robert Palfrey Utter and Gwendolyn Bridges Needham, *Pamela's Daughters* (New York: Macmillan, 1936), 21–23.

22. Clark, *Working Life of Women*, 197 and 235; Hill, *Women, Work, and Sexual Politics*, 51–52. Marlene Le Gates implicitly opposes Clark on this issue in her article, "The Cult of Womanhood in Eighteenth-Century Thought," *Eighteenth-Century Studies* 10 (Fall 1976): 21–39. Le Gates sees the new female ideal as a consequence of Enlightenment ideology, and not as a result of social or economic changes. She bases her argument on recent studies suggesting that women's work patterns remained essentially the same after the Industrial Revolution: see Joan W. Scott and Louise A. Tilly, "Women's Work and the Family in Nineteenth-Century Europe," in *The Family in History*, ed. Charles E. Rosenberg (Philadelphia: University of Pennsylvania Press, 1975), 145–78, and Barbara Ehrenreich and Deirdre English, "The Manufacture of Housework," *Socialist Revolution* 5 (October–December 1975): 5–40. The evidence collected by these scholars, however, refers to a later period in the history of women's labor, to working-class rather than to middle-class women, and to the kind of work done rather than to the economic value and social significance of that work. In fact, the claim that working-class women perform the same kinds of tasks in the seventeenth as in the nineteenth century would not affect the socioeconomic interpretation of the value of women's labor in the eighteenth century. See Hill, *Women, Work, and Sexual Politics*, 24–46.

spouse, further served to exclude married women from participation in the economy. Income, if these women could earn it, would by law not even be their own. Mary Astell, one of the period's most eloquent commentators on the situation of women, describes the marriage contract as a "private Tyrrany":

> Let the Business be carried as prudently as it can be on the Woman's Side, a reasonable Man can't deny that she has by much the harder Bargain: because she puts herself entirely into her Husband's Power, and if the Matrimonial Yoke be grievous, neither Law nor Custom afford her that Redress which a Man obtains. He who has Sovereign Power does not value the Provocations of a Rebellious Subject.[23]

It should be no surprise that the changes that pushed women's labor to the periphery of the economy coincided with an increased urgency to marry, an increased concern and pity for unmarried women, and the appearance of a new victim of ridicule: the spinster.[24] The fate of the female textile worker, and of the term that was originally her occupational designation, graphically illustrates the alteration in the economic status of women. Spinning was traditionally a household industry, dominated by women who produced yarn for their families and for personal sale. With the growth of wage labor, the spinster, previously an essential participant in domestic manufacture, was progressively excluded from productive work, except as a wage-earner in a pauper trade. The currency of "spinster" as a derogatory

23. Mary Astell, *Some Reflections upon Marriage*, 4th ed. (1730; reprint, New York: Source Book Press, 1970), 34–35. For the authoritative account of the patriarchal legal dimensions of women's history in the eighteenth century, see Susan Staves, *Married Women's Separate Property in England, 1660–1833* (Cambridge: Harvard University Press, 1990).

24. Stone, *Family, Sex and Marriage*, 380–86; Utter and Needham, *Pamela's Daughters*, 31–33 and 215–35.

term for a useless female dependent dates from this period of transformation (1719) and records the extent and effect of the changes in the attitude toward women.[25]

The economic phenomena that tended to force the exclusion of middle-class women from the economy were joined with an impetus of another kind, seemingly less coercive, but actually inextricable from the more tangible social changes that it justified and augmented. With the rise of affluence, genteel leisure became the ideal for the wives of well-off tradesmen. The idle female was a badge of status, a proximate sign of gentility, and an ornament for a class whose male members defined themselves in terms of business. Daniel Defoe's typically moralistic lament for the decline of conjugal business participation suggests the prevalence of this new arrangement:

> In former times tradesmens widows valued themselves upon the shop and trade, or the warehouse and trade that was left them . . . . But now the Ladies are above it . . . . The tradesman is foolishly vain of making his wife a gentlewoman, and forsooth he will have her sit above in the parlour, and receive visits, and drink Tea, and entertain her neighbors, or take a coach and go abroad; But as to the business, she shall not stoop to touch it, he has Apprentices and journeymen, and there is no need of it.[26]

The critical response with which this ideal was received shows that it was felt to be radically divergent from the active productive prototype of a previous generation of women:

25. See *OED*; Ian Watt, *The Rise of the Novel: Studies in Defoe, Richardson, and Fielding* (London: Chatto & Windus, 1957), 145; and Clark, *Working Life of Women*, 93–149.

26. Daniel Defoe, *The Complete English Tradesman*, 2 vols. (London: printed for Charles Rivington, 1726), Letter 21, 1:352–55. See also Stone, *Family, Sex and Marriage*, 348–97, and Utter and Needham, *Pamela's Daughters*, 24–25.

Those hours which in this age are thrown away in dress, plays, visits and the like, were employed in my time in writing out receipts or working beds, chairs and hangings for the family. For my part, I have plied my needle these fifty years, and by my good will would never have it out of my hand. It grieves my heart to see a couple of proud, idle flirts sipping their tea, for a whole afternoon, in a room hung round with the industry of their great-grandmother.[27]

The Spectator, an ideological compendium in itself, displays the power of the new female prototype with appropriate complexity: Steele defines the ideal woman as a weak and passive creature, and Addison complains about the idleness, the inanity, and the false fragility of the modern female.[28] The new ideal, evidently, did not go unchallenged. In fact, like many ideologies, it was not universally upheld and applauded. The sign of its vitality and significance is rather that it was assumed to be universal, that it was taken seriously enough to provoke frequent comment and strenuous debate.[29] Thus the withdrawal of women from household labor and the reduction of conjugal business participation were legitimized by a cultural ideal that excluded active or productive enterprise of any kind. The image of the idle female as it spread downward in society reflected,

27. A letter of 1714 printed in *Dear Miss Heber: An Eighteenth-Century Correspondence*, ed. Francis Bamford (London: Constable, 1936), xxii. Also quoted in Stone, *Family, Sex and Marriage*, 348.

28. Richard Steele, *Spectator* no. 144 (15 August 1711), and Joseph Addison, *Spectator* no. 323 (11 March 1712), in *The Spectator*, ed. Donald F. Bond, 5 vols. (Oxford: Clarendon Press, 1965), 2:70 and 3:181–85.

29. Jean E. Hunter in "The 18th-Century Englishwoman: According to *The Gentleman's Magazine*," in *Woman in the 18th Century and Other Essays*, ed. Paul Fritz and Richard Morton (Toronto: Samuel Stevens Hakkert, 1976), 73–78, attempts to challenge the notion of the trivialization of women, which she attributes to Clark, by showing that the conservative ideal of the helpless female was not universal in the periodical literature of the time. In fact the evidence she cites, which points to a lively and continuing debate on the "woman problem," strengthens the argument for a new and necessarily controversial female prototype.

defined, and reified the process of social change, but also confirmed and furthered that process (Stone, *Family, Sex and Marriage*, 397).

Economics and ideology, then, combined to exclude middle-class women from active production, and further rationalized such inactivity as inability to work, constitutional weakness, helplessness, passivity, and stasis. This intricate complex was further elaborated by the central position of the female consumer. Women took on a highly visible role in the new marketplace of the consumer society. Female fashion, in particular, attracted substantial attention in the market and in the cultural realm in general, as did the consumable products of mercantile capitalism—coffee, tea, chocolate, and the accoutrements of the tea table, over which women typically presided.[30] These economic and social changes were accompanied by the concurrent rise of the companionate marriage, and by the related strictures of marital fidelity, devotion, and obedience (Stone, *Family, Sex and Marriage*, 270–81 and 315–404). For the representation of women in the literary discourse of the period, these multiple and multiply interconnected shifts had two related corollaries. The first was the cult of womanhood, which in its fullest development joined chastity, sexlessness, innocence, and moral purity to simple helplessness; the result was a new female paradigm that has persisted over more than two hundred years. The second was the image of the commodified woman, a venerable figure to be sure, but one which acquired a new vitality and relevance in the early eighteenth century. This image had a complicated double life, participating in both a negative and a positive hermeneutic—sometimes simultaneously. Commodification

30. See McKendrick, "The Consumer Revolution of Eighteenth-Century England," in McKendrick, Brewer, and Plumb, *The Birth of a Consumer Society*.

was often the basis for an attack on women, as Swift's and Pope's treatment of female figures amply demonstrates. But the female paragon herself could be a figure of commodification, like Pamela dressing in her country clothes, and counting the objects from her mistress that she carries away in her little bundle or the money from Mr. B that she will distribute to her ex-fellow servants. Indeed, as we shall see in connection with the theme of dressing in Pope's aesthetic writing, the ideal female cultural arbiter was made the object of and rationale for trade in contemporary Whig panegyric poetry. Thus though the helpless woman and the commodified woman usually take separate paths in the literature of the period, and though they seem almost incompatible with each other, they belong to the same cultural configuration. The helpless and victimized woman functions through an economically enforced gender division as a figure of difference; the commodified woman as a figure for the mystery of fetishization.

The appearance of the defenseless protagonist in the drama of the late seventeenth and early eighteenth centuries, then, is not an isolated aesthetic incident. It represents an early literary version of the new female prototype—passive, pathetic, but not always chaste or sexless—a figure of profound significance not only for the image of women in the period, but also for the contemporary ideological problematic of accumulation, commodification, and even empire. Indeed, this pathetic female figure provides a way of integrating an influential contemporary construction of female sexuality with mercantile imperialist ideology, a way of articulating a private proposition about sexuality with a massive and world-historical political enterprise.

Thus, the significance of the pathetic female figure of the she-tragedy is shaped by the economic insignificance of real women in eighteenth-century history. Richardson's Mr.

B defines the social and cultural lack of status of the new female prototype with characteristic precision: "A Man enobles the Woman he takes, be she *who* she will; and adopts her into his own Rank, be it *what* it will: But a Woman, tho' ever so nobly born, debases herself by a mean Marriage, and descends from her *own* Rank, to *his* she stoops to."[31] Women, in short, take on the social valuation of their husbands; they have no inherent valuation of their own. Without a male figure to define her status, a woman is an empty vessel. And as such, in the drama of the period she facilitates a complex ideological process that involves sexuality and commodification as well as the repudiation of aristocratic class hierarchies, the institution and celebration of bourgeois ideals, the programmatic representation of violence against women, and the promulgation of the cult of womanhood.

Because she is apparently located outside of any class hierarchy—aristocratic or bourgeois—the statusless woman of the she-tragedy can stand formally and generically between the representation of an aristocratic ideal of chivalric magnanimity and a didactic bourgeois ideal of moral worth. In this regard, the she-tragedy bridges the gap between intrinsically irreconcilable forms. It emerges directly from the seventeenth-century heroic play and comes to repudiate the essential premises of that drama. It does so, however, not by breaking with the explicit class hierarchies of aristocratic form, but by allowing them to lapse into an evaluative vacuum through the figurative vacuity of the female victim. The affective plight of its suffering heroine is subsequently tagged with ethical significance and thus translated, with equal seamlessness, into the moral context of bourgeois

31. Samuel Richardson, *Pamela, or Virtue Rewarded*, 4 vols. (Stratford-upon-Avon: Basil Blackwell, Oxford, for the Shakespeare Head Press, 1929), 2:253.

tragedy.[32] Lillo himself cites the affective form of the late Restoration as the necessary enabling precursor to *The London Merchant*:

> The Tragic Muse, sublime, delights to show
> Princes distrest, and scenes of royal woe:
> In awful pomp, majestic, to relate
> The fall of nations, or some hero's fate
>
> . . . .
>
> Upon our stage, indeed, with wish'd success,
> You've sometimes seen her in a humbler dress,
> Great only in distress. When she complains
> In Southerne's, Rowe's, or Otway's moving strains,
> The brilliant drops that fall from each bright eye
> The absent pomp, with brighter gems, supply.
> Forgive us then, if we attempt to show,
> In artless strains, a tale of private woe.
>
> (prologue to *The London Merchant*, lines 1–20)

The final pleasure of the she-tragedy—that misogynist pleasure to be found in the pain of the female victim—substitutes a common outpouring of sympathy, a community of sentiment, for a stable system of values based on an aristocratic class hierarchy. Sentiment thus serves, through misogyny, as the basis of a reassuring unity in a period of class instability.

As we have seen, in this very process of embodying female devaluation and of enabling the transition to a bourgeois form, the she-tragedy makes a proposition about sexuality: that female sexuality and female bodies are constituted by victimization, violence, and suffering. Such a

32. Eugene Waith's "Tears of Magnanimity in Otway and Racine," in Eugene Waith and Judd D. Hubert, *French and English Drama of the Seventeenth Century* (Los Angeles: William Andrews Clark Memorial Library, University of California, 1972), 1–22, documents this continuity from a different perspective.

proposition implies a perverse and problematically indistinguishable relationship between pleasure and pain, between licit and illicit sexual activity, and even between masculine and feminine sexuality, that raises a question about
the nature of sexuality in general. And indeed, the problem of a stable sexuality is evident in the proliferation of
contradictions that we have observed in this drama: between the passive and the sexually powerful woman, the
orphan and the promiscuously connected woman, the innocent would-be virgin and the radically sexualized agent of
social destruction. Thus although the attack on the female
protagonist asserts a misogynist community of interest as a
substitute for class identity, it simultaneously asserts a particular constitution of sexuality as well. That is, the pleasure
taken in the violation and death of the female protagonist
sets up a new, powerful identity of affect through which
the audience of the drama can construct for themselves a
stable, mutually accepted form of sexuality. Since this form
of sexuality is defined in relation to the female victim,
or rather, more specifically, in terms of violence against
women, it is constitutionally masculine, though not necessarily exclusively male. By this means, the complex phenomenon of that premier bourgeois cultural form, the cult
of sensibility, could be described, at least in its earlier
stages, as the affective process by which an unstable class
identity is negotiated away and the notion of a knowable
and controllable female sexuality—and by extension of a
stable sexuality in general—is constructed through a figurative redaction of the major shift in the social and economic position of women effected by the rise of mercantile
capitalism. But the problem of sexuality does not end here.

We have noted that the representation of sexuality as victimization is one early consequence of the process of the
economic devaluation of women; commodification is just a
later stage of that same process—the stage at which the

middle-class woman, already effectively withdrawn from production, becomes the prototypical consumer. In this context, the translation of sexuality into commodification that we observed in *Jane Shore* indicates the relationship between these two stages in the process of the economic and social positioning of women in the period, just as it also indicates the nature of the generic transition from aristocratic to bourgeois form. Both female passivity and female commodification involve an emptying out of significance that projects the economic devaluation of women into literary culture, facilitates the development of a moralized drama of bourgeois virtue out of a chivalric form, and thus consolidates that economic devaluation and that generic transition by inscribing it in the cult of womanhood and its affective cousin, the cult of sensibility.

From this perspective, the violence directed against the passive and commodified woman can be seen as something more than misogyny. If, as I have suggested, the female figure in these plays condenses two of the significant social dimensions of the rise of mercantile capitalism—the economic devaluation and the commodification of women, then the numerous actual and contemplated rapes in the she-tragedy serve in part as a form of unconscious resistance to that historical process through which the figure of the woman is constituted in this period. And indeed the cursing and the apocalyptic despair that characterizes the climactic episodes of the she-tragedy confirm this sense of an impassioned rejection of contemporary society. These curses typically refer to the experience of inevitable misfortune that defines the cruel worlds of these plays: "Confusion and disorder seize the world, / To spoil all trust and converse amongst men . . ."; "Final destruction seize on all the world! . . . / Crush the vile globe into its first confusion; / Scorch it with elemental flames to one cursed cinder, / And all us little creepers in't, called men, / Burn, burn to nothing."[33] In this sense, ironically, rape and resistance may be perversely allied.

Reading the domestic she-tragedy—this simpleminded drama of despair and hysterics—as a major generic example of the feminization of mercantile capitalist ideology gives us a means of integrating a large complex of formal problems and ideological propositions—a way of connecting categories as diffuse as affect, commodification, and labor, as critically distinct as generic development and ideological transition, as distant from each other as sexuality and economics, and as incompatible with each other as rape and resistance. Such an integration necessarily points in many directions at once, and the critical model proposed by this reading similarly seeks to open lines of inquiry and articulation, particularly in exploring the dynamic negotiations between history and sexuality embodied in these plays. But these articulations also include a definition of the nature of the discursive and ideological connection between violence and commodification, an examination of the position of labor and economy in relation to constructions of sexuality or to accounts of generic transition, and an interpretation of the cult of sensibility in terms of rape or resistance. On a larger scale, the conjunctions built on such inquiries might connect students of sexuality and especially of gay and lesbian culture with Marxist, materialist, or political critics. And such connections, at the least, might let us see the scope and fertility of the figure of the woman in eighteenth-century literary culture, the range of her reference, the versatility of her ideological role. At the most, they might enable us to shape from that versatility new forms of articulation among political or radical critical projects.

33. Thomas Otway, *The Orphan*, V.516; *Venice Preserved*, ed. Malcolm Kelsall (Lincoln: University of Nebraska Press, 1969), V.ii.93–98.

4

Capitalizing on Women:
Dress, Aesthetics,
and Alexander Pope

> On the contrary, one may represent true Wit by the Description which *Aristinetus* makes of a fine Woman, when she is *dress'd* she is Beautiful, when she is *undress'd* she is Beautiful: Or, as *Mercerus* has translated it more Emphatically, *Induitur, formosa est: Exuitur, ipsa forma est.*
>
> Joseph Addison, *Spectator* no. 61

If we read the aesthetic theory of the early eighteenth century for its attention to classical models, its concern with hierarchies and rules, or its consistent appeal to authority, order, and decorum, we would be unlikely to encounter the issues of gender or empire. Aesthetic theory, after all, is typically represented as a realm unto itself by contemporary practitioners and modern commentators alike. And indeed early eighteenth-century aesthetic theory, perhaps the most canonical of the discourses about art in English literary culture, itself provides the model for the separation of the spheres of art and history, art and politics, or art and empire. This implied distance from history, whether social, political, or economic, makes aesthetic theory an ideal subject for a strong reading of the status of imperialist ideology in this period, and of the crucial role of gender in the constitution of that ideology. Strong, because such a reading will have to contend with the modern edifice of explication and appreciation that maintains the assumption of a self-sufficient and self-generating aesthetic discourse in this period; but also because in claiming to account for a discursive field so seemingly separate from history, such a reading will be making a proposition about the hegemonic nature of imperialist ideology, about the imaginative priority and the cultural operation of a powerful, pervasive contemporary account of experience.

Though part of the enterprise of this essay is to show the inseparability of aesthetics and politics, part of its analytical advantage lies in this relative isolation of aesthetic discourse. In its own assertion of self-sufficiency, aesthetic theory is secluded from the most obvious or evident connections with history, whether in the form of political allusion, historical topicality, allegorical reference, or even a narrative shape against which the processes of experience or identity can be tried. As a result of this self-appointed seclusion, the pressures of history upon aesthetic discourse are likely to be at least once removed; they must be mediated through an ideological category that holds them at a distance from the realm of art. I argue here that in eighteenth-century aesthetic writing, history is mediated most consistently through the category of gender; in particular that the figure of the woman is the discursive means to the connection of imperialism and aesthetic theory, that the role of that figure also raises related questions about sexuality, and that eighteenth-century aesthetics provides an ideal context in which to observe the functional relationship of gender and empire. Thus the recalcitrant context of aesthetics gives us an opportunity to isolate a powerful ideological process and to view the correlative workings of gender and empire in the self-attested purity of the realm of art.

Even the standard summaries of eighteenth-century literary criticism—although they describe and classify notions of authority, decorum, and rules—implicitly encourage us to read in a different direction. According to R. S. Crane, the enterprise in this period of setting out the just and proper standards of poetry is consistently based upon a conjunction of "opposite qualities," an arrangement that—though it has in prospect a version of the classical mean by which all contradictions are resolved—entails in practice a kind of sustained tension, a permanent irresolution, and, as Crane says, a discourse characterized by "manipulations of contrarities, or of positive and privative terms."[1] Among Crane's examples of this sort of manipulation is Pope's famous couplet:

> *True Wit* is *Nature* to Advantage drest,
> What oft was *Thought*, but ne'er so well *Exprest*.[2]

William K. Wimsatt and Cleanth Brooks see in this same aphorism "a kind of minimum classical stand, a last-ditch defense of wit-theory after a century more or less of the

1. R. S. Crane, "English Neoclassical Criticism: An Outline Sketch," in *Critics and Criticism: Ancient and Modern*, ed. R. S. Crane (Chicago: University of Chicago Press, 1952), 380–81.

2. Alexander Pope, *Essay on Criticism*, I.297–98. All references to Pope's poetry are to *The Twickenham Edition of the Poems of Alexander Pope*; vol. 1, *Pastoral Poetry and An Essay on Criticism*, ed. E. Audra and Aubrey Williams (London: Methuen; New Haven: Yale University Press, 1961); vol. 2, *The Rape of the Lock and Other Poems*, ed. Geoffrey Tillotson (London: Methuen; New Haven: Yale University Press, 1940); vol. 3, bk. 2, *Epistles to Several Persons (Moral Essays)*, ed. F. W. Bateson (London: Methuen; New Haven: Yale University Press, 1951); and vol. 4, *Imitations of Horace with An Epistle to Dr Arbuthnot and The Epilogue to the Satires*, ed. John Butt, 2d ed. (London: Methuen; New Haven: Yale University Press, 1953).

empirical assault." Like Crane, they also find here a tension, irresolution, or manipulation characteristic of the otherwise apparently stable and prescriptive assertions of aesthetic norms in early eighteenth-century criticism. But they place these tensions in the context of the seventeenth-century decline of rhetoric. For Wimsatt and Brooks "the cleavage in the art of verbal expression," the breakdown of the system of classical rhetoric, and the ultimate subordination of the word to the idea, of form to content, stand behind Pope's paradoxical couplet.[3]

Pope's definition of "True Wit" can serve as the type of this pervasive and symptomatic problem in eighteenth-century aesthetic thought. The separation of "Wit" and "Nature" into two incommensurate categories is in itself an ominous sign for the reputation of rhetoric. But beyond this, Pope's couplet is systematically uninformative. Though not a part of "Nature," "True Wit" seems to have an indispensable role in representation. But at the same time the couplet implies a subordination or trivialization of language as merely an elegant form of "expression," which stands in contrast to a more essential, originary "Nature" located either in the classical models, in human reason as it imitates the divine, or in a general, universal order. Whether "Wit" fundamentally alters or merely embellishes this "Nature," to what extent "Nature" maintains its significance apart from "Wit," and how the inconclusive invocation of "Advantage" operates to arbitrate their connection—these questions are raised and kept open, rather than laid to rest, in Pope's problematic prescription.

The significant ambiguity at the heart of Pope's proposition is illustrated more concretely in the toilet scene of *The Rape of the Lock* (1711, 1714, 1717), in which Belinda, wor-

3. William K. Wimsatt and Cleanth Brooks, *Literary Criticism: A Short History* (New York: Random House, 1957), 242 and 226.

shiping in the mirror the "heav'nly Image" (I.125) that supplies her inspiration and her model, produces a representation of beauty that participates both in nature and in artifice at once:

> Now awful Beauty puts on all its Arms;
> The Fair each moment rises in her Charms,
> Repairs her Smiles, awakens ev'ry Grace,
> And calls forth all the Wonders of her Face;
> Sees by Degrees a purer Blush arise,
> And keener Lightnings quicken in her Eyes.
>
> (I.138–44)

Again, necessary ornamentation and unadorned nature are systematically confounded. What Belinda sees in the mirror is paradoxically both her undressed self and the fully elaborated idea of a general nature that her artifice can only approximate. And that artifice seems both to constitute the beauty that emerges in the passage—in this sense there is no unadorned original—and at the same time merely, in a manner subsidiary and trivial, to heighten or embellish qualities already present in "Nature."

The attempt to understand this ambiguity as a consequence of the decline of classical rhetoric, or the rise of empiricism, or the allegiance to an ideal of the classical mean, or a complex combination of all these factors, is of course characteristic of the kind of explanation dominant in histories of literary criticism. The motive force of change, for Wimsatt and Brooks or R. S. Crane, is to be found in ideas themselves; for the purpose of their arguments, the most relevant form of history is literary and intellectual history. Without rejecting the accounts of these historians of ideas, we can find another explanation for the problematic of "True Wit," an explanation arising from the relationship between literary culture and the material conditions of eighteenth-century society. Using Pope as the prototype, and focusing on the symptomatic ambiguity residing in the tension between the word and the idea, or between Belinda's natural beauty and her artificial adornment, I would like to pursue the problematic of literary criticism in the first half of the eighteenth century in a direction different from that taken by Crane or Wimsatt and Brooks, in the direction of gender and empire.

The impact of the bourgeois revolution in the seventeenth century, and of the shift to a money economy and the rapid growth of mercantile capitalism in the eighteenth—these major, decisive political, economic, and social changes provide another context for the ambivalent ornamentalism of eighteenth-century poetic theory. Indeed, one could argue that such changes supply the motive for that whole complex of forces in the intellectual context that is commonly seen as responsible for eighteenth-century aesthetics; in other words, that the attraction of a non-contradictory, classical middle way, the rise of empiricism, the influence of the plain style, and the attack on rhetorical extravagance are all connected to major and pervasive social and economic changes. But whether or not we believe that a materialist account can wholly subsume an idealist one, and however we rank the various factors in the process of mediation by which literary culture finds its conditions of possibility in history at large, the new, predominantly capitalist economic system of eighteenth-century England certainly informs the ambiguous definition of the proper standards of literature in the aesthetic theory of Pope and his contemporaries, both through changes in intellectual orientation, and through the direct pressure of the world of commodities on the world of art.

The metaphor of dressing, which Pope uses in the *Essay on Criticism*, *The Rape of the Lock*, and—as we shall see—

throughout his poetry to describe the status of artifice in relation to essence, is no casual, innocent, or idiosyncratic verbal decoration. In fact, it appears repeatedly as a natural and almost automatic trope in this period for the role of rhetoric. In a precursor to the *Essay on Criticism*, the verse *Epistle to a Friend concerning Poetry* (1700), Samuel Wesley turns to the same typical image:

> *Good Sense* is spoil'd in Words *unapt exprest*,
> And *Beauty* pleases more when 'tis *well drest*.[4]

Wesley is more reductive and abrupt than Pope. For him "Style is the *Dress* of *Thought*," a dress that should be modest, neat, "not *gaudy* . . . nor a worse Extream / All daub'd with *Point* and *Gold* at every Seam" (*Epistle* lines 138–41). Edmund Waller, in his verses introducing Roscommon's translation of Horace's *Ars Poetica*, "Of this Translation, and of the Use of Poetry" (1680), employs not only the same metaphor but the same rhyme that marks the later aphoristic pronouncements of Wesley and Pope:

> *Brittain*, whose Genius is in Verse exprest
> Bold and sublime, but negligently drest.[5]

"Dressed/expressed" has the status, in the period of Waller and Pope, of what Hugh Kenner calls a "normal rhyme," a rhyme that convinces its readers that it represents a connection natural and inherent to "the workings of a normal mind." According to Kenner, this "feel of the normal" has its source in literary convention—for example, in the linkages of key words authorized by their recurrent connection

---

4. Samuel Wesley, *Epistle to a Friend concerning Poetry*, lines 348–49, (1700; reprint, Ann Arbor, Mich.: Augustan Reprint Society, 1947), 10.

5. Edmund Waller, "Of this Translation, and of the Use of Poetry," preface to *Horace's Art of Poetry*, translated by the Earl of Roscommon (London, 1680).

in pastoral or biblical traditions.[6] But what seems most significant in "dressed/expressed" as a tenet of "the workings of a normal mind" in this period is not so much its connection with literary history, but rather the distinctive and unexpected context of gender and even of sexuality that it evokes.

Charles Gildon, in the preface to his influential treatise *The Complete Art of Poetry* (1718), advertises his intention to practice a new method of familiar discourse, to bring the rules of poetry "by a pleasing and familiar Dress to the Capacity of a Lady, who had not any Learning, and nothing but good Sense to direct her."[7] Perhaps this admirable goal accounts for the unacknowledged, lengthy paraphrase of Sidney's *Apologie for Poetrie*—in "that easie Address, which . . . wou'd gratifie the *Goust* of the *Ladies*" (*Complete Art of Poetry* 101) that takes up a large part of Dialogue 1. The preoccupation with women surfaces strikingly in Gildon's revision of Sidney's eloquent image: "Nature neuer set forth the earth in so rich tapistry as diuers Poets have done."[8] In Gildon's words, "Nature never adorn'd the Earth in so rich and charming a Dress as several of the *Poets* have done" (*Complete Art of Poetry* 50). The contrast between Sidney's organic "tapistry," an integrative and textured figure that enables the earth to be represented or "set forth" by the poet, and Gildon's ornamental "dress," an external "adornment" for an underlying essence, compactly illustrates the fragmented status of literary representation in early eighteenth-century criticism, in which a problematic or derogatory incommensurability between the word

6. Hugh Kenner, "Pope's Reasonable Rhymes," *ELH* 41 (1974): esp. 76–78.

7. Charles Gildon, *The Complete Art of Poetry* (1718; reprint, New York: Garland, 1970), preface to vol. 1.

8. Philip Sidney, *An Apologie for Poetrie*, in *English Literary Criticism: The Renaissance*, ed. O. B. Hardison (New York: Appleton-Century-Crofts, 1963), 104.

and the idea becomes a governing assumption. This tension seems to hold a special fascination for eighteenth-century aestheticians, a fascination that the "normal" "dressed/expressed" image plays out. Repeatedly in these formulations, "dressing" evokes an implied contrast with the undressed or the naked. The Jonathan Richardsons (father and son), in *Remarks on Milton's Paradise Lost* (1734), come directly to the point: "Were I called upon to Define Poetry in General . . . I would do it by saying 'tis ORNAMENT. . . . for Dress, Lace, Gold, Jewels, & c. is not the Body."[9] The second dialogue of Gildon's *Complete Art of Poetry*, which includes a debate between two women on the ubiquitous subject of the relationship between wit and poetry, displays this "Body" with even more sexual specificity: "And as for your Ladyship's *fine Things*, and *fine Language*, to prefer these to more charming, and more essential Excellencies, wou'd be as ridiculous, as to prefer your Ladyship's *Dress* to your Person" (107).

Indeed, the naked female body is barely concealed behind this metaphor of aesthetic formulation. We can uncover it further in Fielding's playful allegory in *The Champion* (1739) of a trip to Parnassus to meet the muses, whose formal Greek names are shortened to familiar contemporary equivalents, perhaps also for the benefit of an unlearned female audience:

> On one of the summits of this Hill sat nine Girls, whose Names I learnt to be Miss *Cally*, Miss *Cly*, Miss *Raty*, Miss *Thally*, Miss *Pomy*, Miss *Psicky*, Miss *Terpy*, Miss *Polly*, Miss *Any*; they were very indifferently dressed, but so extremely beautiful, that the Rents in their Garments, which discover'd some

9. Jonathan Richardson [father] and Jonathan Richardson [son], *Explanatory Notes and Remarks on Milton's Paradise Lost*, in *English Literary Criticism, 1726–1750*, ed. S. J. Sackett (Hays, Kansas: Fort Hays Kansas State College, Fort Hays Studies, n.s., Literature Series 1, 1962), 59.

parts of their charming Limbs, would have been ill supply'd by the richest Brocade.[10]

"The workings of a normal mind" in this period, at least as reflected in the "dressed/expressed" rhyme, seem to include a special concern with the adornment of the female body. The implicit and explicit voyeurism, the question of the status of ornament, of gold and jewels or "rich Brocade," in relation to the "charming Limbs" or the "charming, and . . . essential Excellencies" of the undressed female figure, and above all the drive to uncover some underlying, essential, and untransmutable female nature—these connected and ubiquitous obsessions form the context for one of the central tenets of aesthetic thought in the early eighteenth century.

The image of female dressing and adornment has a very specific, consistent historical referent in the early eighteenth century—the products of mercantile capitalism. The association of women with the products of trade is a strong cultural motif in this period, and the concern with female adornment and particularly dress is a prominent expression of that association. In fact, Neil McKendrick's study of the commercialization of English culture designates dress and fashion as the century's prototype for commodification. As McKendrick says, "Clothes were the first mass consumer products to be noticed by contemporary observers." "Fashion and dress are often used almost interchangeably. From Mandeville on special attention was given to the role of clothes in this process of social and economic change."[11]

10. Henry Fielding, *The Champion*, 13 December 1739, in *The Champion* (London, 1741), 1:88.
11. Neil McKendrick, "The Commercialization of Fashion," in Neil McKendrick, John Brewer, and J. H. Plumb, *The Birth of a Consumer Society: The Commercialization of Eighteenth-Century England* (Bloomington: Indiana University Press, 1982), 53 and 51.

The implicit cultural designation of dress as a synecdoche for commercialization is not surprising, since one of the earliest economic sources of the expansion and capitalization of the English economy was the textile industry, specifically the wool trade. So central was this notion, that Defoe cited dress quite literally as the primary basis of English imperialism: for him English prosperity began with the textile industry, and would be sustained by the spread of English cloth around the world. He even fantasized that the civilizing powers of English culture would bring clothing to the naked Africans, thereby promoting civilization, dress, and the English economy all at once: "there needs little more than to instruct and inure the barbarous Nations . . . in the Arts of Living; clothing with Decency, not shameless and naked. . . . [This would raise] an immense Consumption of our Woolen Manufactures, where there was little or no Consumption for them before."[12]

The Rape of the Lock supplies the locus classicus of this theme. Belinda is not only dressed, she is "deck'd with all that Land and Sea afford" (V.11). And her toilet scene makes the economic context of the trope of female adornment explicit: the artifice through which Belinda's beauty is either created or awakened is attributed to the products of trade and defined through a catalogue of commodities for female consumption:

> Unnumber'd Treasures ope at once, and here
> The various Off'rings of the World appear;
> From each she nicely culls with curious Toil,
> And decks the Goddess with the glitt'ring Spoil.

12. Defoe, *A Plan of the English Commerce* (London, 1728), 338, 348. According to Peter Earle ("The Economics of Stability: The Views of Daniel Defoe," in *Trade, Government and Economy in Pre-Industrial England,* ed. D. C. Coleman and A. H. John [London: Weidenfeld & Nicolson, 1976]), "Millions of Africans, now ashamed of their nakedness, would regularly demand suit of bays and English stocking" (280).

> This Casket *India*'s glowing Gems unlocks,
> And all *Arabia* breathes from yonder Box.
> The Tortoise here and Elephant unite,
> Transform'd to *Combs*, the speckled and the white.
>
> (I.129–36)

Throughout the literary culture of this period, tortoise shell and ivory, the spices of Arabia, gems, gold, and silk are made to represent the primary objectives of mercantile capitalism, and these commodities in turn appear exclusively as the materials of the female toilet and wardrobe. The misogynist satire of this period, as we shall see in our reading of Swift's writings on women in Chapter 6, typically takes the form of an inversion of the celebratory commodification of women exemplified in this imperialist apologia. For Swift too, the dressing of the female body is the crucial issue, and what lies under the dress, whether "charming Limbs" or something much less attractive, is the crucial focus of attention.

This ideological fixation on female dress and adornment is expressed with the most direct vehemence by Bernard Mandeville in his description of the operations of a prosperous capitalist economy in *The Fable of the Bees* (1724). Associating female luxury quite directly with economic stimulation, Mandeville takes the petticoat, an epitome of conspicuous consumption, as a test case for his economic theory; he describes "the silly and capricious Invention of Hoop'd and Quilted Petticoats" as one of the most important changes in English history, barely surpassed in significance by the Reformation.[13] Elsewhere, in a more general vein, he argues at length "that a considerable Portion of what the Prosperity of *London* and Trade in general, and

---

13. Bernard Mandeville, *The Fable of the Bees: or, Private Vices, Publick Benefits*, ed. F. B. Kaye (Oxford: Clarendon Press, 1924), 2 vols., I:356. Subsequent references will be to this edition.

consequently the Honour, Strength, Safety, and all the
worldly Interest of the Nation consist in, depends entirely
on the Deceit and vile Stratagems of Women" in their consumption of a "vast quantity" of trinkets and apparel, which
they "come at by . . . pinching their Families . . . and other
ways of cheating and pilfering from their Husbands," and
by "ever teazing their Spouses, tire them into Compliance,"
or "by downright Noise and Scolding bully their tame Fools
out of any thing they have a mind to." For Mandeville "Humility, Content, Meekness, Obedience to reasonable Husbands, Frugality, and all the Virtues together, if they
[women] were possess'd of them in the most eminent Degree, could not possibly be a thousandth Part so service-
able, to make an opulent, powerful, and what we call a
flourishing Kingdom, than their most hateful Qualities,"
that is, the taste for luxury, "the Consumption of Super-
fluities" (*The Fable of the Bees* I.225–28). It is interesting that
this account of female commodification is subtly linked to a
corollary concern with the nature of female sexuality:

> the Young and Beautiful especially laugh at all Remon-
> strances and Denials, and few of them scruple to employ the
> most tender Minutes of Wedlock to promote a sordid Interest
> [in commodities]. Here had I time I could inveigh with warmth
> against those Base, those wicked women, who calmly play their
> Arts and false deluding Charms against our Strength and Pru-
> dence, and act the Harlots with their Husbands! Nay, she is
> worse than Whore, who impiously prophanes and prostitutes
> the Sacred Rites of Love to Vile Ignoble Ends; that first ex-
> cites to Passion and invites to Joys with seeming Ardour, then
> racks our Fondness for no other purpose than to extort a
> Gift, while full of Guile in counterfeited Transports she
> watches for the Moment when Men can least deny. (I.227–
> 28)

For Mandeville, the problem, or the threat, or the ambiguous nature of female sexuality thus arises in connection

with the issue of commodification in a way that echoes the significant conjunction that we traced in Chapter 3 between the sexualized female victim and the female object of mercantile adornment.

Joseph Addison, like Mandeville, also takes up the issue of the petticoat, but in a more panegyrical strain. In a *Tatler* paper in which the petticoat is brought to judgment and defended for its contribution to the "improvement of the woollen trade" and "the benefit which . . . thereby accrue[s] to" the "Greenland trade . . . [through its] great consumption of whalebone," Addison ends with a typical statement of the necessary connection of women and adornment:

> I consider Woman as a beautiful Romantick Animal, that may be adorned with Furs and Feathers, Pearls and Diamonds, Ores and Silks. The Lynx shall cast its Skin at her Feet to make her a Tippet; the Peacock, Parrot, and Swan, shall pay Contributions to her Muff; the Sea shall be searched for Shells, and the Rocks for Gems; and every Part of Nature furnish out its Share towards the Embellishment of a Creature that is the most consummate Work of it."[14]

Addison's female figure disappears behind or within or beneath the numerous treasures and rarities with which she is adorned, and all of nature seems to cooperate in this process of adornment and erasure. Of course, the collaboration represented here is only a rationalized version of imperialist expansionism. In the discourse of early eighteenth-century mercantile capitalism this is the most common trope of all, by which the agency of the acquisitive subject and the urgency of accumulation are concealed and deflected through the fantasy of a universal collaboration in the dressing of the female body.

14. Joseph Addison, *Tatler* no. 116 (5 January 1709–10), in *The Tatler*, ed. Donald F. Bond, 3 vols. (Oxford: Clarendon Press, 1987), 2:125.

In this context, our "dressed/expressed" image has a specific historical location. But we can be even more precise in describing its function in connecting women and empire. The discourse of the imperialist trope of dressing is marked by a characteristic, even obsessive, repetition of a rhetorical figure: that of anaphora. We glimpsed this figure briefly in our discussion of the commodification of Jane Shore in Chapter 3, "For whom the foreign vintages were pressed, / For whom the merchant spread his silken stores."[15] The initial repetition of "for whom" is a discursive product of the deflection of agency typical of the trope of dressing, urgently and redundantly claiming to locate the motive force of the whole enterprise of mercantile capitalism in the female figure who consumes its products instead of in the male who profits from her consumption. The same anaphora recurs in the same context in many other works of imperialist apologia in this period: "For them the Gold is dug on Guinea's coast . . . / For them Arabia breathes its spicy Gale," "For you the silkworms fine-wrought webs display . . . / For you the sea resigns its pearly store."[16] The women indicated by "for them" and "for you" and "for whom" in the anaphora running through this poetry are identified not only with the products of mercantile capitalism, but also with the whole male enterprise of commerce

15. Nicholas Rowe, *The Tragedy of Jane Shore*, V.i.111–17, in *British Dramatists from Dryden to Sheridan*, ed. George H. Nettleton and Arthur E. Case (Boston: Houghton Mifflin, 1939).

16. James Ralph, *Clarinda, or the Fair Libertine: A Poem in Four Cantos* (London, 1729), 37–38; Soame Jenyns, *The Art of Dancing. A Poem* (1730), in *Poems* (London, 1752), 7. Both *Clarinda* and *The Art of Dancing* are quoted in Louis A. Landa, "Pope's Belinda, the General Emporie of the World and the Wondrous Worm," *South Atlantic Quarterly* 70 (1971): 223 and 232. In a discussion of Pope's *Essay on Man* in my *Alexander Pope* (Oxford: Basil Blackwell, 1985), 75–78, I provide another, more extended, account of this structure of initial repetition, linking it to the epistemological problems in that poem.

that generates those commodities. Indeed, a reversal of object and agent becomes naturalized in the use of this trope. It is as if navigation, trade, and expansion are all arranged solely for the delectation and profit of womankind. Women wear the products of accumulation, and thus by metonomy they are made to bear responsibility for the system by which they are adorned. The activities and motives of male mercantilists and the systematic, bureaucratic, piratical, or mercenary dimensions of imperial expansion disappear behind the figure of the woman, who is herself subsumed by the products that she wears.

In the closing lines of *Windsor Forest* (1713), Pope uses the same rhetoric of reversal to avoid his own implication in imperialist brutality and capitalist acquisition. Here he contemplates the profits that will result from the new English mercantile supremacy initiated by the Peace of Utrecht:

> For me the Balm shall bleed, and Amber flow,
> The Coral redden, and the Ruby glow,
> The Pearly Shell its lucid Globe infold,
> And *Phoebus* warm the ripening Ore to Gold.
>
> (393–96)

"For me" expresses all the acquisitive energies of the mercantile capitalist entrepreneur, all the fascination with accumulation, exploitation, and possession that characterizes an imperialist culture. But again the agency of acquisition is suppressed; no one need own this covetousness. The first person pronoun, though of course it directly voices the hegemonic imperialist commitment of the culture, is actually spoken by Father Thames, who, like the female referent of "for you," "for them," and "for whom," serves as a proxy through which the drive for acquisition can be articulated without indicating its beneficiary.

The trope of dressing, then, has two connected implications. Mercantile capitalism itself, with all of its attractions as well as its ambiguous consequences, is attributed to women, whose marginality allows them to serve, in the writings of celebrants and satirists alike, as a perfect proxy or scapegoat. And perhaps even more important, female adornment becomes the main cultural emblem of commodity fetishism. In Marxist thought, the "mystical character of the commodity"[17] arises with the generalization of commodity exchange, when the physical products of human labor become confounded with human beings themselves. This substitution occurs because, under an advanced system of exchange, products acquire their value not from their utility, but through their potential for exchange with other products. Under these conditions, "the commodity reflects the social characteristics of men's own labour as objective characteristics of the products of labour themselves, as the socio-natural properties of these things. Hence it also reflects the social relation of producers to the sum total of labour as a social relation between objects, a relation which exists apart from and outside the producers" (Marx, *Capital*, vol. 1, 164–65). As exchange value comes to usurp use value, and relations between things replace relations between people, human beings themselves can come to be redefined as objects. The "secret" or the mystery, then, that the fetishism of the commodity always conceals is the real structure of human relationships underlying those values dictated by exchange, "the definite social relation between men themselves which assumes . . . the fantastic form of a relation between things" (165). This period in English history is characterized by precisely that extension of exchange—in the form of mercantile capitalism—that Marx

17. Karl Marx, *Capital*, trans. Ben Fowkes, vol. 1 (New York: Random House, 1977), 164.

describes as the condition for the fetishism of commodities. But more specifically, the figure of the woman, because of her connection with the material products of accumulation, comes to embody the whole complex question of the real human relations that underlie the fantastic ones created by commodification. That is, through images of dressing and adornment, women become a cultural focal point for the representation of the commodity, and thus by association they become a primary locus for the ideological problem of fetishization. In this sense, the "enigmatic character" of the commodity (164) is represented, in early eighteenth-century literary culture, by the problematic female figure. And the obsessive and ambiguous dressing and undressing of that figure can be seen as an attempt to strip away the mystifying "clothing" of the commodity and to discover the lost human essence that lies beneath.

In short, the undressing of women represents a serious reflection on the mystery of commodity fetishism by a culture in the early stages of commodification. Such a reflection, and the recurrent discursive evocation of female dressing upon which it depends, is a distinctive characteristic of this period. Later in the eighteenth century, when the process of commodification is more advanced, this cultural concern to penetrate the mystery of the commodity is largely lost. But even here, the sustained and diverse explorations of dress and undress raise the problem of fetishization rather than resolving it. As we shall see in Chapter 6, Swift's concern to strip the female body of all its clothes only produces a more essentially fetishized figure. Indeed, a resolution of this mystery is by definition impossible: commodification arises as a cultural crisis precisely because the fundamental social relations between people become impenetrable. Thus, early eighteenth-century aesthetics, with its sustained tension between nature and art, thinks in terms of the structural categories of commodity fetishism, but it does not strictly juxtapose nature and art on the one hand with use value and exchange value on the other. It is caught in the realm of exchange, and from there it absorbs and reflects some of the major questions and heterodoxies of the period.

Perhaps the most extensive and revealing treatment of dressing in the poetry of this period occurs in Pope's *Sober Advice from Horace* (*Second Satire of the First Book of Horace*, 1734). This poem gives us an opportunity to explore the dynamic of the naked and the dressed more intensively, and to read, through its many intertextual connections with Pope's explicitly aesthetic writings, the numerous conjunctions among the trope of dressing, the problem of female sexuality, the question of sexual identity, the process of commodification, and the problematic of early eighteenth-century aesthetic theory with which we began. As an "imitation" of Horace, the *Second Satire* belongs to the contemporary engagement with the cultural materials of the age of Roman imperialism. Pope's explicit practice, much like Dryden's, was to provide a contemporary equivalent to the classical texts, a cultural rather than a literal translation. This enterprise necessarily involves a process of interpretation in which the canonical materials of the classical period are recruited in the service of a contemporary ideological project.[18] In this case, Pope chooses for its contemporary relevance a Horatian poem that raises the issue of female sexuality in relation to male taste, and "imitates" Horace by presenting that issue in terms of our familiar metaphor of dress and undress.

At its 1738 publication, the poem was retitled *A Sermon against Adultery, Being Sober Advice from Horace*. It announces its topic at its outset: the elusive and ambiguous nature of

18. I have described the ideological significance of Pope's neoclassicism more fully in relation to *The Rape of the Lock* in the first chapter of my *Alexander Pope*.

122 Ends of Empire

female sexuality. "All the Court" laments the death of "dear charming *Oldfield*," a contemporary actress and sex symbol who, "with Grace and Ease, / Could joyn the Arts, to ruin, and to please" (5–6). Following this evocation of a public example of the exploitation of female sexuality are a series of other portraits: of a well-known prostitute, "*Con. Philips* . . . [for whom] 'Treat on, treat on,' is her eternal Note, / And Lands and Tenements go down her Throat" (11–14); of "*Fufidia*" who "With all a Woman's Virtues but the P–x, / . . . thrives in Money, Land, and Stocks: / For Int'rest, ten *per Cent.* her constant Rate is; / Her Body? hopeful Heirs may have it *gratis*" (17–20); of "*Rufa* [who is] at either end a Common-Shoar" (29); and of "*Peg*" than whom "Nothing in Nature is so lewd . . . , / Yet, for the World, she would not shew her Leg!" (31–32).

The speaker summarizes the import of these images of female avarice, appetite, and duplicity in the aphorism that states the poem's "Theme": "Women and Fools are always in Extreme" (28). As sexual objects, these women present so many problems that the poem advocates, as its central satiric tenet, that men shift their sexual interest from aristocratic and publicly renowned women to the lower classes and the common prostitute: "How much more safe, dear Countrymen! his State, / Who trades in Frigates of the second Rate?" (61–62). This class bias dominates the body of the poem, and it is represented consistently by our "normal" dressing image. Midway through the satire, Pope, altering Horace in order to highlight the motif of dress and undress, describes this preference for a woman of humbler rank, who will undress to show her wares, to a lady of quality, who will always remain fully clothed:

> *First*, Silks and Diamonds veil no finer Shape,
> Or plumper Thigh, than lurk in humble Crape:
> And *secondly*, how innocent a *Belle*

Is she who shows what Ware she has to sell;
Not Lady-like, displays a milk-white Breast,
And hides in sacred Sluttishness the rest.

(106–11)

These lines contain the typical eighteenth-century attack on
women for hypocritical and perhaps filthy concealment, an
attack that we will explore more fully in our discussion of
Swift. But Pope's ability to opt for nakedness here, in the
liberated and iconoclastic context authorized by satiric
form, enables him to redeem, relatively and conditionally,
at least one segment of the gender. This option is unavail-
able to Pope in more misogynist moments—all the women
in the *Epistle to a Lady* remain fully clothed.

The *Second Satire* continues with a lengthy fantasy of
stripping, deflected into a horse-trading metaphor that
Pope again alters from Horace to focus attention on the
matter of undressing rather than dressing:

Our ancient Kings (and sure those Kings were wise,
Who judg'd themselves, and saw with their own Eyes)
A War-horse never for the Service chose,
But ey'd him round, and stript off all the Cloaths;
. . . .
A Lady's Face is all you see undress'd;
(For none but Lady M–– shows the Rest)
But if to Charms more latent you pretend,
What Lines encompass, and what Works defend!
. . . .
Could you directly to her Person go,
Stays will obstruct above, and Hoops below,
And if the Dame says yes, the Dress says no.

(112–32)

Even the woman is in conflict with her dress here, as the
material object with which she is adorned takes on a sepa-

rate life and speaks on her behalf, or rather contradicts her
speech with its own. But the real spokesman for this obsession with the naked and the dressed is an animated penis,
the only one that I have noticed in Pope's corpus:

> Suppose that honest Part that rules us all,
> Should rise, and say—"Sir *Robert!* or Sir *Paul!*
> "Did I demand, in my most vig'rous hour,
> "A Thing descended from the Conqueror?
> "Or when my pulse beat highest, ask for any
> "Such Nicety, as Lady or Lord *Fanny?*
>
> (87–92)

The "poor Suff'rer" (94) stands up here to voice his objec-
tion to the erroneous and elitist preference for the lady of
quality whose "Dress says no" when the woman in "humble
Crape" is willing to "strip off all the Cloaths" and offer her
wares without pretense, delay, or obstruction. And the
speaker here further associates that erroneous elitism with
a confusion of sexual preference; "Lord *Fanny*" (John,
Lord Hervey, often attacked for his effeminate manner-
isms)[19] is made to seem interchangeable with the reprehen-
sible "Lady" whose dress makes her sexually inaccessible.
Both that "Lady" and "Lord *Fanny*" are implicitly rejected
as objects that the "honest part" never sought out; the
penis's very honesty makes such pretentious "Niceties" an-
athema. But in fact, the question of sexual preference or
sexual practice is connected with the problem of female
sexuality even in those opening descriptions of public lewd-
ness: "Lord Fanny" appears in the second line of the poem,
as one of Oldfield's mourners. And into that initial group

19. On the contemporary use of Hervey in connection with the evocation of sexual deviancy, particularly sodomy, hermaphroditism, and what
we would now call homosexuality, see Jill Campbell, "Politics and Sexuality
in Portraits of John, Lord Hervey," *Word and Image* 6 (1990): 281–97.

of portraits, Pope smuggles a vivid image suggestive of sodomy that turns on a perverse superimposition of breasts
and buttocks, when "bashful *Jenny*, ev'n at Morning-Prayer,
/ Spreads her Fore-Buttocks to the Navel bare" (33–34).[20]

At this point, the figure that we have traced from the
"dressed/expressed" rhyme to the trope of the naked and
the dressed and the contemporary representation of female
commodification has collected an interconnected constellation of categories, including gender, sexuality, and class, as
well as the issue of artifice and essence. The problematic
role of the ambiguous ornamentalism that characterizes
aesthetic discourse is represented as both a sexual and a
class ambivalence. Just as the artifice of wit obtrudes upon
the essential beauty that is the true poet's aesthetic objective, dress obstructs the function of a "natural" and properly directed sexuality, and it unjustly promotes aristocratic
privilege by enabling women of quality to conceal their
"sluttishness." Under the aegis of Horatian irony, which enables this text to both own and disown this iconoclasm,
Pope moves toward the heart of the "mystery" concealed by
dress and in the process passes through the major heterodoxies of class leveling and unconventional sexual practice.

That concealment or obstruction is the focus for a com-
plaint of a seemingly different sort elsewhere in Pope's poetry. In the *Epistle to a Lady* (1735), following the sarcastic
portrait of Queen Caroline, Pope raises the same concern:

> Poets heap Virtues, Painters Gems at will,
> And show their zeal, and hide their want of skill.
> 'Tis well—but, Artists! who can paint or write,
> To draw the Naked is your true delight.
> That Robe of Quality so struts and swells,

20. I am grateful to Gordon Turnbull for calling my attention to this
passage.

> None see what Parts of Nature it conceals.
> Th' exactest traits of Body or of Mind,
> We owe to models of an humble kind.
> If QUEENSBERRY to strip there's no compelling,
> 'Tis from a Handmaid we must take a Helen.
>
> (185–94)

Unskillful poets cover their subjects with the "Gems" or "Silks and Diamonds" (*Second Satire*) of the well-dressed woman of quality, but the true "Artist," like the penis, prefers "the Naked"; for him too the "Handmaid" or the woman in "humble Crape" supplies the ideal and "exactest object," in this case a moral as well as an aesthetic and sexual ideal. These passages from Pope illustrate the fluid reciprocity between the categories of gender and aesthetics that marks the currency of the "dressed/expressed" metaphor in this period. The problem is more elaborately articulated, and we must move between poems to define it, but it only develops what we have already seen in Gildon's simple statement that to prefer *"fine Language"* to substance is like preferring "your Ladyship's *Dress* to your Person."

We can return now to the *Essay on Criticism* and the argument surrounding the famous couplet with which we began. The poem's aesthetic project, to define "True Wit" through an explication of the reciprocal relation between criticism and poetry, is founded upon a sustained allusion to the teleological experience of bourgeois and mercantile imperialist English history, in particular in the constitutive conjunction of liberty and law:

> Those RULES of old *discover'd*, not *devis'd*,
> Are *Nature* still, but *Nature Methodiz'd*;
> *Nature*, like *Liberty*, is but restrain'd
> By the same Laws which first *herself* ordain'd.
>
> (88–91)

Nature, poetry, criticism, and society are efficiently superimposed in this allusion to the founding tenet of capitalist social theory. And this connection of poetic and social liberty is sustained in the long course of the poem through allusions to the Gothic origins of parliamentary government (649–50, 715), to the improper absolutist "*Licence*" of Charles II's era (681–84), and especially to the expansionist destiny of the *pax Britannica*, figured through the neoclassical lens of Roman imperialism:

> Thus long succeeding Criticks justly reign'd,
> *Licence* repress'd, and *useful Laws* ordain'd;
> *Learning* and *Rome* alike in Empire grew,
> And *Arts* still *follow'd* where her *Eagles flew*.
>   (681–84)

In short, Pope's most abstract aesthetic statement cannot, even in its largest premises, be separated from the ideological structures of contemporary mercantile capitalism, and these structures suggest the context in which its aesthetic argument is already situated.[21] Its local evocations of wit, nature, poetry, criticism, and ornament, however, belong even more evidently to the constellation of themes that we have discerned in relation to the "dressed/expressed" trope of early eighteenth-century commodity fetishism.

The passage on "diff'rent *Styles*" (322), for example, is based on a sustained analogy to dress and fashion:

> Expression is the *Dress* of *Thought*, and still
> Appears more *decent* as more *suitable*;
> A vile Conceit in pompous Words exprest,
> Is like a Clown in regal Purple drest . . . .
> In *Words*, as *Fashions*, the same Rule will hold;
> Alike Fantastick, if *too New*, or *Old*;

21. Here I am very briefly summarizing my argument about the ideological basis of *The Essay on Criticism* in my *Alexander Pope*, chap. 2. That more substantial account is also more attentive to the contradictions in Pope's construction of English history.

> Be not the *first* by whom the *New* are try'd,
> Nor yet the *last* to lay the *Old* aside.
>
> (318–36)

And the lines that precede the famous paradigmatic statement on "True Wit" make the by now familiar transition from dress to nakedness:

> Poets like Painters, thus, unskill'd to trace
> The *naked Nature* and the *living Grace*,
> With *Gold* and *Jewels* cover ev'ry Part,
> And hide with *Ornaments* their *Want of Art*.
> *True Wit* is *Nature* to Advantage drest,
> What oft was *Thought*, but ne'er so well *Exprest*.
>
> (293–300)

The same "*Gold* and *Jewels*," the same "*Ornaments*," and the same fascinating state of undress play the same central metaphorical role here as they do in the *Second Satire* and *To a Lady*.

In fact, we can trace in the juxtaposition of these three poems—the *Second Satire*, *To a Lady*, and the *Essay on Criticism*—the process of abstraction by which the trope of the naked and the dressed is sublimated: from the woman in "humble Crape" who is the object of a "natural" heterosexual attraction, to the portrait of the ideal woman, which exactly traces the inner traits of "Body or of Mind" through its basis in a "naked" model, to the enterprise of "True Wit," which is said to supersede ornamentation despite its necessary ornamentalism. This process of sublimation brings us again to the symptomatic tension between artifice and essence that pervades the aesthetic discourse of this period. If we turn it on its head, we can see this process as one of distillation or materialization rather than sublimation, by which the problematic ideal of "True Wit" is objectified as an assertion of the heterosexual desires of the "honest

Part," and the tensions of aesthetic theory are vested in the
anxieties about sexuality raised by the elusive or duplicitous
operations of female dress and adornment. This way around,
the sexual ambivalence in the trope of the naked and the
dressed is equated with the problematic of aesthetic theory.
Indeed, reading the *Essay on Criticism* against the *Second Satire* highlights this very equation. In the latter poem the ambiguous image of Jenny's "Fore-Buttocks" is immediately
succeeded by an evocation of divergent sexual preferences:
"But diff'rent Taste in diff'rent Men prevails, / And one is
fired by Heads, and one by Tails" (35–36). In the *Essay* the
counterpart passage refers not to sexual but to aesthetic
difference and stylistic suitability: "For diff'rent *Styles* with
diff'rent *Subjects* sort, / As several Garbs with Country,
Town, and Court" (322–23). In this context, the assertion
of a "natural" sexual desire based on an enforced heterosexuality is embedded in the unrealizable aim of the resolution of the problematic of aesthetic theory. Either as sublimation, or materialization, or both, the true artist speaks
for the penis and vice versa; what the poet contemplates in
the act of true art is the same as what the penis wants in a
woman; the obsession with the naked and the dressed is the
metaphorical pivot on which the connection between gender and aesthetics turns.

The fantasy of female nakedness authorized by the penis's
words, which occupies the body of the *Second Satire*, is reversed at the end, in a passage without a specific precedent
in Horace. Pope describes an ideal rendezvous with his
"willing Nymph" (161) and the "deep Tranquility" (175) of
such direct and simple satisfaction. But at least one current
of his sexual fantasy life seems to run in a different direction. The purportedly "humble" class of his ideal female
figure is contradicted immediately in the epithets with
which the poet praises her: "*Angel! Goddess!*" (166). And,
perversely, he imagines that "solid Happiness" (145) nega-

tively, at length, in terms of an alliance with a woman of quality and the interruption and subsequent furious disturbance that would have been attendant upon such an affair:

> No furious Husband thunders at the Door;
> No barking Dog, no Household in a Roar;
> From gleaming Swords no shrieking Women run;
> No wretched Wife cries out, *Undone! Undone!*
> Seiz'd in the Fact, and in her Cuckold's Pow'r,
> She kneels, she weeps, and worse! resigns her Dow'r.
>
>   (167–72)

And at the center of all this distressing attention:

> Me, naked me, to Posts, to Pumps they draw,
> To Shame eternal, or eternal Law.
>
>   (173–4)

At this point, we might want to ask who is naked and who is dressed in this concluding variation upon our "normal" "dressed/expressed" image. The more familiar candidate for nakedness, of course, is the female body, as we have seen, but our trope can apparently extend its purview to men as well. Or rather, in this case, the naked male body suddenly and quite unexpectedly emerges from a context that so far has focused only on naked women. In the climactic lines of this poem, it is the male poet's state of dress or undress that is actually the center of attention and anxiety. The naked women whom the poet has contemplated earlier fade from focus in the face of this urgent evocation of male undress. In fact, in retrospect, those naked women seem to have only been proxies for a naked man: or rather, their ambiguous state of dress or undress indicates the poet's ambivalence about his own sexuality, his futile attempt to avoid the anxiety of his own nakedness and to remain decorously dressed during his own sexual fantasies.

The female body, then, takes the place of the male body, and in this place serves as a locus for the enactment of a male anxiety about sexuality. This anxiety includes the penis's earlier evocation of sodomy and its assertion of a "natural" rejection of sexual heterodoxy, and it is linked to the ambiguous attack on class status and the preference for a "humble" object of heterosexual desire. That is, the attempt to undress the female body uncovers a complex male dilemma in which a variety of normative propositions and orthodoxies are suddenly made unstable. By this logic, aesthetic theory too can be seen in terms of a contemporary and historical male anxiety. The notion of "True Wit," as I have argued here, is wedded—for better and for worse—to the female image of *naked Nature*" and the "models of an humble kind." As a pervasively feminized figure, then, "True Wit," like the alternately dressed and undressed female body, stands in the place of a male problematic, in a structural reversal that we shall see repeated elsewhere in the literary culture of this period.

The trope of the naked and the dressed provides a point of access to a significant and complex dimension of early eighteenth-century imperialist ideology. It arises from the specific connection of the image of female dressing with trade and commodification, and in its own sustained discursive ambivalences it explores the tensions and the mysteries of fetishization. Though nakedness might seem the ideal model, especially from the point of view of the penis in the *Second Satire*, the crucial quality of this trope is its ambiguity, its symptomatic inability to see through the dress to that naked ideal despite its purported preference. Even the penis describes the beauties of his ideal object negatively and comparatively in terms of the clothing that covers it: "Silks and Diamonds veil no finer Shape, / Or plumper Thigh, than lurk in humble Crape."

As the grounding image of aesthetic writing, the trope of the naked and the dressed reveals the process of sublimation by which the mysteries of fetishization are constituted as the defining problematic of ornamentalism in eighteenth-century aesthetics. Ornament and nature are in the same ambiguous relation as dress and undress: "True Wit" arrives to dress nature to advantage at precisely the moment when she is stripped naked in the critique of the unskilled poet. We can observe the operation of this dynamic in yet another context in the *Epistle to Burlington*, in which the penis and the true artist are replaced by the landscape gardener:

> To build, to plant, whatever you intend,
> To rear the Column, or the Arch to bend,
> To swell the Terras, or to sink the Grot;
> In all, let Nature never be forgot.
> But treat the Goddess like a modest fair,
> Nor over-dress, nor leave her wholly bare;
> Let not each beauty ev'ry where be spy'd,
> Where half the skill is decently to hide.
>
> (47–54)

This passage bares and dresses the body of the pseudo-mythical female figure in the same breath. The question of how much to dress and how much to bare, like the question of the relationship of "Wit" to "Nature" in the aphorism from the *Essay on Criticism*, remains unanswered. The perpetual state of ambiguity that characterizes the relation between "Wit" and "Nature," word and idea, dress and undress, replays the mystification of commodity fetishism, the increasing indistinguishability of thing and essence, commodity and human being. This conjuncture Marx described as the period of the relative immaturity of fetishization: "As the commodity-form is the most general and the most undeveloped form of bourgeois production, it makes its appearance at an early date, though not in the same predominant and therefore characteristic manner as nowadays. Hence its fetish character is still relatively easy to penetrate" (*Capital,* vol. 1, 176). In this respect, the transitional status that Wimsatt and Brooks see in Pope's "last-ditch" defense of rhetoric has its parallel in the transitional status of early eighteenth-century economy and culture.

In expressing the unresolvable mystery of fetishization, the trope of the naked and the dressed also exposes the ideological intimacy of female sexuality and commodification, an intimacy that we began to trace in the translation of sexuality to adornment in *Jane Shore.* The question of the essential nature beneath the dress, the engagement with undress and nakedness, and the representation of an unknowable or threatening female sexuality, all indicate a correspondance between the tensions of gender difference and those of commodification. The struggle to know the female body and to understand and control female sexuality is in this sense a corollary to the struggle with the process of alienation imposed by commodification. Both these struggles are doomed to fail, but they open up other tensions along the way. In the undressing of the female figure, nakedness is temporarily connected with an attack on social status, and in the examination of the mysteries of female sexuality, conventional sexual practices and even the assumption of a "natural" heterosexuality are briefly and locally destabilized. Thus in the literary culture of this period, the tensions surrounding sexuality and class identity—ongoing contemporary crises themselves—intersect with the interconnected categories of gender, empire, and aesthetics.

In its conjoined evocation of commodification and sexuality, the trope of the naked and the dressed is structurally implicated in the process of displacement or reversal by which mercantile capitalism is naturalized, rationalized, and ambiguously affirmed. Indeed, the ambiguities and anxieties of this transitional period seem to be concentrated in the figure of the woman, who stands for the whole complex and unresolvable problem posed by the early history of capitalism. The strange exchangeability of male for female bodies that we observed at the end of the *Second Satire*, and the deflection of agency that we have seen to be a corollary to the commodification of women—these seemingly anomalous discursive moves are the rhetorical signs of the ideological proposition that women bear responsibility for empire, and they represent the mechanism by which the culture disposes of the contradictions of the dominant ideology, the tensions inherent in mercantile capitalism. But those contradictions cannot be wholly repressed. They are evident, as we have seen, in the "cleavage" in the structure of early eighteenth-century aesthetic theory, in the obsessive and repetitive turn in the literary culture of this period to women, dress, and undress, and in the related flirtation with unconventional sexual activities and the brief attack on elitist class allegiances. In this sense, the representation of women is the locus for the intersection of empire and aesthetics in this period, and in that role the figure of the woman supplies a place where some of the most troubling questions of the age are repeatedly raised.

5

Amazons and Africans:
Daniel Defoe

> But suffer not thy Wife abroad to roam:
> If she love Singing, let her Sing at home;
> Not strut in Streets, with *Amazonian* pace,
> For that's to Cuckold thee, before thy Face.
> . . . .
> For, if she holds till her nine Months be run,
> Thou mayst be Father to an *Ethiop's* Son:
> A Boy, who ready gotten to thy hands,
> By Law is to Inherit all thy Lands:
> One of that hue, that shou'd he cross the way,
> His Omen wou'd discolour all the day.
>
> John Dryden, *The Sixth Satyr of Juvenal*

In this chapter I use a reading of a powerful trope in the representation of women as the basis for an exploration of the discursive relation between gender and empire in early eighteenth-century literary culture. The title "Amazons and Africans" refers more to the aim of connecting the categories of race and gender than to the actual balance between these two categories in the course of my argument. I focus here mainly on Amazons—in eighteenth-century literature variously and in Defoe's *Roxana* (1724) at some length. Recently, the figure of the Amazon has attracted the attention of feminist theorists and cultural historians, as well as classicists, anthropologists, and literary critics; and Amazons have been seen variously as emblems of female

autonomy, figures of myth, examples of misogyny, or the-
matizations of romantic heroism.[1] In literature, outside the
classical, the traditional critical focus on the figure of the
Amazon has been on the drama and epic of the Renaissance;[2] the Amazon has not been seen as an active figure in
the literary culture of the eighteenth century. I hope to
show, however, that the Amazon—or the threatening, autonomous woman that this figure epitomizes—is a significant image in the representation of difference in this period; that she is most readily perceived and most usefully
understood specifically in terms of contemporary representations of exchange, accumulation, and commodification;
and finally that the Amazon is for this period an important
form of mediation in the representation of imperialist ideology.

By focusing on Defoe, one of the most prolific and eloquent apologists for mercantile expansion in early eighteenth-century literary culture, I stand in the place of the
imperialist, and view the "other" from the perspective of
the dominant ideology. This perspective inevitably places
gender before race, because gender represents a category
of difference constituted primarily within the geographical

1. For example, Page duBois, *Centaurs and Amazons: Women and the
Pre-History of the Great Chain of Being* (Ann Arbor: University of Michigan
Press, 1982); Abby Wettan Kleinbaum, *The War Against the Amazons* (New
York: McGraw-Hill, 1983); Sharon W. Tiffany and Kathleen J. Adams,
The Wild Woman: An Inquiry into the Anthropology of an Idea (Cambridge,
Mass.: Schenkman, 1985); William Blake Tyrrell, *Amazons: A Study in
Athenian Mythmaking* (Baltimore: Johns Hopkins University Press, 1984);
Julie Wheelwright, *Amazons and Military Maids* (London: Pandora Press,
1989).

2. See Simon Shepherd, *Amazons and Warrior Women: Varieties of Feminism in Seventeenth-Century Drama* (New York: St. Martin's Press, 1981);
Stephen Orgel, "Jonson and the Amazons," in *Soliciting Interpretation: Literary Theory and Seventeenth-Century English Poetry*, ed. Elizabeth D. Harvey
and Katharine Eisaman Maus (Chicago: University of Chicago Press,
1990), 119–39.

purview of the dominant culture, whereas the understanding of race in this period, despite the increasing visibility of
non-European racial groups in England, remains mainly
extrinsic, geographically foreign, a category of difference
defined as an external object. For that reason, in this chapter I come to the African through the Amazon; in the concluding section I use Defoe's image of the African in *Captain Singleton* (1720) as a test case for the connection of the
representation of difference with the ideology of empire.

The final question I ask here is whether or to what extent taking the perspective of the imperialist and placing
gender analytically before race forces us to adopt the hierarchies of empire. Does such a perspective systematically
block access to forces of subversion, resistance, or autonomy outside the range of imperialist thought? These questions are directly relevant to the exploration of the feminization of mercantile capitalist ideology in relation to slavery,
colonialism, or racial difference in the chapters on Behn
and Swift. In this context, I would like to return to the
issue that I raised in Chapter 1, of the political implications
of this study, and in particular of the relation between my
approach and that of recent new historical or Foucauldian
or "political" criticism. As I have suggested, my aim is to
propose a self-conscious political agenda for a criticism focusing on the relationship between literature and society.

Such an agenda must seek to define a progressive or radical political criticism. My central assumption is that "political" criticism stands its best chance of finding a progressive
use if it attends to issues of inequity and exploitation as
they arise in literary history in such a way as to further the
struggle to end such conditions in our own period: that is,
if it is oriented at least partly toward recovering liberationist positions, or if it provides us with a means of demystify-
ing and then challenging a seemingly monolithic oppressive
discourse. In this chapter I attempt both to recover the ex-

pression of a socially critical position and to uncover the functioning of an oppressive ideology by reading symptomatically a figure of subordination and difference. That is, I claim to find in my account of Amazons and Africans a dual progressive use—both a positive model and negative lesson.

One of the most disturbing images in Juvenal's sixth satire, a work that served as an influential model for the representation of women in eighteenth-century England, is not so much the famous figure of the lady in her dressing room, though we shall return later to that trope, but rather the one that depicts female soldiers and gladiators, the description of the women at their military exercises. This is Dryden's translation:

> In every Exercise the Mannish Crew
> Fulfils the Parts, and oft Excels us too:
> Prepar'd not only in feign'd Fights t' engage,
> But rout the Gladiators on the Stage.
> . . . .
> Behold the strutting *Amazonian* Whore,
> She stands in Guard with her right Foot before:
> Her Coats Tuck'd up; and all her Motions just,
> She stamps, and then Cries hah at every thrust,
> But laugh to see her tyr'd with many a bout,
> Call for the Pot, and like a Man Piss out.[3]

In part Juvenal's effect here depends on a simple comic gender reversal: the woman playing the man's role. The laughter is rather brief, though, and the image conceals more anxiety than mere ridicule would warrant. The figure

3. John Dryden, *The Sixth Satyr of Juvenal*, lines 350–70, in *The Poems of John Dryden*, ed. James Kinsley (Oxford: Clarendon Press, 1958). Subsequent references to Dryden's Juvenal will be to this edition.

of the woman who "thrives on masculine violence" ("quae figut a sexu, vires amat"),[4] either by practicing it directly or by associating herself with men who do so, appears in a variety of forms throughout Juvenal's long and diffuse poem. She is the one who joins the rough crew of sailors, braving the difficult and dangerous voyage to Alexandria, to elope with a gladiator. It is of her that Juvenal says "ferrum est quod amant" (113): the sword is what they love, or in Dryden's words:

> But 'twas his Fencing did her Fancy move;
> 'Tis Arms and Blood and Cruelty they love.
>
> (157–58)

That same "ferrum" returns in the last lines of the poem, when women become the most horrific of "Fiends," a whole sex that will coolly commit murder for money—subtly, with poison, if that is most convenient, or brutally, with the sword. These days:

> Where e're you walk, the *Belides* you meet; [these are fifty sisters who killed their fifty husbands on their wedding night]
> And *Clytemnestras* grow in every street.
>
> (854–55)

This movement from laughter to violence is characteristic of Juvenal's attack on women. As Dryden's translation puts it, with the typical neoclassical emphasis on generic distinctions, the satire slips into tragedy:

> You think this feign'd; the Satyr in a Rage
> Struts in the Buskins, of the Tragick Stage.

4. This is Peter Green's translation of Juvenal's lines 355–56 in *Juvenal: The Sixteen Satires* (Harmondsworth, Middlesex: Penguin, 1967).

Forgets his Bus'ness is to Laugh and Bite;
And will, of Deaths, and dire Revenges Write.
Wou'd it were all a Fable, that you Read.
(828–32)

The image of the armed and warlike woman is the agent of this generic transformation. She provides the point where comic transvestism turns to tragic violence, the apocalyptic telos and the serious message of Juvenal's misogyny.

These murderous women are described as springing directly from the money, luxury, and peace of the Roman empire:

But wanton now, and lolling at our Ease,
We suffer all th' invet'rate ills of Peace;
And wastful Riot, whose Destructive Charms
Revenge the vanquish'd World, of our Victorious Arms.
(405–8)

In short, the Amazons are a direct consequence of the *pax Romana*. Although politically women were marginal to the construction of the Roman or the British empire, culturally the constellation of discourses that served to represent the initiation, consolidation, celebration, defense, and even the critique of imperialism is intimately involved with the representation of women—in Rome as in early eighteenth-century England—and the manlike, murderous woman plays a crucial role in this discourse.

The image of the warlike or murderous woman that we find in Juvenal supplies a model for the trope of the Amazon in early eighteenth-century literary culture. This trope was evidently a resonant one in the period, and a variety of writers turned repeatedly to Juvenal's misogynistic satire as a model and an inspiration. Dryden's translation had seven printings between 1692 and 1735. But the poem was also translated by Henry Fielding in 1725, by Edward Burnaby

Greene in 1763, and by Edward Owen in 1785.[5] Fielding rendered Juvenal's verse in Hudibrastics and with contemporary references that brought the problem of the threatening Amazon up to date:

> Have you not heard of fighting Females,
> Whom you would rather think to be Males?
> Of Madam *Sutton*, Mrs. *Stokes*,
> Who give confounded Cuts and Strokes?
> They fight the Weapons through complete,
> Worthy to ride along the Street.[6]

Fielding refers to Mrs. Sutton, a female prize fighter of the day, and to Elizabeth Stokes, another genuine female gladiator, who fought at both boxing and quarterstaff in public bouts at London amphitheaters.[7]

In a study of "gender and identity" in Fielding's works, Jill Campbell finds the rebellious, warlike, unnaturally aggressive woman to be a figure of central relevance at various stages in Fielding's career. Campbell argues that gender reversal and the concomitant problem of "petticoat government" substantially shape Fielding's plays. And she shows that *Tom Jones* is significantly informed by a connection with Fielding's attack on Jacobitism, an attack that in contemporary accounts of the '45 focused on the Jacobite reversal of proper, hierarchical relations between the sexes, and most vividly upon the claim that the Jacobite movement was dominated by insubordinate, henpecking women, who took up arms and male military garb and went into

5. See Felicity A. Nussbaum, *The Brink of All We Hate: English Satires on Women, 1660–1750* (Lexington: University of Kentucky Press, 1984), 78.

6. Henry Fielding, "Juvenalis Satyra Sexta," lines 364–69, in *Miscellanies by Henry Fielding, Esq.*, vol. 1, ed. Henry Knight Miller (Oxford: Clarendon Press, 1972), 111.

7. Ibid., 111 n. 4. See William B. Boulton, *Amusements of Old London* (London: Nimmo, 1901), 30–31.

battle beside or instead of their husbands in the prince's cause.[8]

In a different context, Dianne Dugaw has argued that a widespread cultural fascination with fighting females characterizes the social life and popular literature of this period. She sees such female prize fighters as Sutton and Stokes—among others—along with the appearance of actual female soldiers in male dress, the interest in female physical vigor and social independence, and the obsession with cross-dressing in fashion, masquerade, and disguise, as an indication of a fundamental and ongoing questioning of gender roles. Dugaw has canvassed the numerous appearances of woman warriors in the street ballads, theatrical interludes, prose biographies, and "histories" of the period. She argues that this topic, long a popular subject in lower-class ballads, moves to a middle-class format and finds a larger and more sophisticated audience in the eighteenth century. These narratives are characterized by a fascination with gender reversal, transvestism, and the notion of female heroism.[9] *The Female Soldier; or, The Surprising Life and Adventures of Hannah Snell* (1750) recounts the career of a woman who in search of her husband took up male disguise and became a soldier, fought with apparent bravery in several battles, and was even seriously wounded without betraying her gender. Snell's enlistment in pursuit of her husband is a common convention in the ballad literature about the female soldier, as well as in the Juvenalian tradition, in which the "Amazonian whore" goes to sea in pursuit of her gladiator lover. The opening passage of Hannah Snell's story suggests the ideological investments that might lie behind this popular woman warrior:

8. Jill Campbell, *Natural Masques: Gender and Identity in Fielding's Plays and Novels* (Palo Alto: Stanford University Press, 1993), chaps. 1, 5, and 6.
9. Dianne Dugaw, *Warrior Women and Popular Balladry, 1650–1850* (Cambridge: Cambridge University Press, 1989).

[The author describes first] this dastardly Age of the World, when Effeminacy and Debauchery have taken Place of the Love of Glory, and that noble Ardor after warlike Exploits, which flowed in the Bosoms of our Ancestors, genuine Heroism, or rather an extraordinary Degree of Courage, are Prodigies among Men. . . . [and through this condemnation of the present age, he introduces the alternative of Hannah Snell's conduct in battle] tho' Courage and warlike Expeditions, are not the Provinces by the World allotted to Women since the Days of the *Amazons*, yet the female Sex is far from being destitute of Heroism.[10]

Dugaw speculates that the female heroism that proved so fascinating in this period of almost continuous warfare might have called contemporary male heroism into question (*Warrior Women* 213–15). And indeed, in this passage Hannah Snell is quite explicitly defined as a heroic female alternative to a contemporary male depravity; her exploits evoke both the anti-heroism of the present-day male soldier and a kind of proxy heroism portrayed by the woman warrior. This role, as we shall see, connects the popular Amazon with the more canonical figures of fighting females in the period.

Aside from their appearance in the Juvenalian and the popular traditions, armed women also appear in the periodical literature of the eighteenth century. Addison in the *Spectator* papers supplies a thumbnail sketch of a society of female warriors in which "no Woman was to be married till she had killed her Man,"[11] and Johnson translated a French text (by the Abbé de Guyon) as *Dissertation on the Amazons* and speculated in the *Idler* on the possibility of a nation of

10. *The Female Soldier; Or, The Surprising Life and Adventures of Hannah Snell* (1750), intro. by Dianne Dugaw, Augustan Reprint Society no. 257 (Los Angeles: William Andrews Clark Memorial Library, University of California, 1989), 1–2.

11. Joseph Addison, *Spectator* no. 434 (18 July 1712), in *The Spectator*, ed. Donald F. Bond, 5 vols. (Oxford: Clarendon Press, 1965), 4:24–26.

warlike women conquering men (Nussbaum, *The Brink of All We Hate*, 44). These references suggest the ways in which the Amazon was part of the culture's peripheral vision; women are not always or even often seen as Amazons, but Amazons haunt the frontiers of the representation of women at various levels and in various modes of discourse.

Perhaps the most canonical version of the trope occurs in the neoclassical format of Pope's *Rape of the Lock*. We have already seen that poem's implication in the contemporary expansion of English commerce and prosperity. But those explicit images of empire are joined with a related, Juvenalian representation of the fighting, militarized female. In this context, one might best describe *The Rape of the Lock* as a displacement of the *Aeneid*, the song of "arms and the man" and of the founding of the Roman empire, onto the figure of the "woman who thrives on masculine violence." Virgil's poem is a representation of continuous warfare, of unrelenting, unmitigated, and ultimately horrific "masculine violence" evoked ambivalently as a retrospective justification and apologia for imperial Rome. Pope's poem echoes Virgil's not only in the numerous details of rhetoric and event so familiar to the neoclassicist sensibility—the machinery of the gods, the journey to the underworld—but also in its structure of repetition, in the obsessive proliferation of scenes of battle, violence, and conquest. In this regard, the Amazon trope is the poem's central metaphor, even though the one actual act of aggression is committed by a man. Belinda "puts on all [her] Arms"[12] in canto 1, and engages in skirmishes and "Murders"(V.145) through the last lines of the poem. Dryden's *Aeneid* stands behind all these battles. The card game at Hampton Court is pre-

---

12. Alexander Pope, *The Rape of the Lock*, I.139, in *The Rape of the Lock and Other Poems*, ed. Geoffrey Tillotson (London: Methuen, 1940). Subsequent references to this poem will be to this edition.

sented in the language of Aeneas's campaigns against the Latins. In Dryden, for instance:

> Now dying Groans are heard, the Fields are strow'd
> With falling Bodies, and are drunk with Blood:
> Arms, Horses, Men, on heaps together lye:
> Confus'd the Fight, and more confus'd the Cry.
>
> . . . .
>
> O Mortals! blind in Fate, who never know
> To bear high Fortune, or endure the low![13]

And in Pope's poem:

> *Clubs, Diamonds, Hearts,* in wild Disorder seen,
> With Throngs promiscuous strow the level Green.
> Thus when dispers'd a routed Army runs,
> Of *Asia*'s Troops, and *Africk*'s Sable Sons,
> With like Confusion different Nations fly,
> Of various Habit and of various Dye.
> The pierc'd Battalions dis-united fall,
> In Heaps on Heaps; one Fate o'erwhelms them all.
>
> . . . .
>
> Oh thoughtless Mortals! ever blind to Fate,
> Too soon dejected, and too soon elate!
>
> (III. 79–86 and 101–2)

Redundantly, like the *Aeneid,* the poem replays this battle scene, with all of its elaborate epic metaphor and its allusions to empire, with the figure of Belinda at its center.

The familiar toilet scene, which echoes Juvenal's influential dressing-room passage, sets up another version of the conjunction of women and empire. Here, Belinda equips herself for battle, and the image of the "woman who thrives on masculine violence" is seen also as the self-consciously

13. John Dryden, *Aeneid,* XI.941–44 and X.698–99, in *The Poems of John Dryden.*

self-adorned female figure. The "Arms" (I.139) that Belinda puts on are the commercial spoils of imperialist expansion. Indeed, as we have seen elsewhere, trade pervades the poem; the tea-table itself and the ubiquitous presence of coffee and tea are a signal of this engagement with mercantile prosperity: according to Defoe's *Review*, "*Coffee, Tea, and Chocolate* . . . it is well known are now become the Capital Branches of the Nations Commerce."[14] The Amazon here is a product and emblem of empire, in her person and in her Virgilian battles. Pope's poem, like Juvenal's, uses the murderous female figure—in which mercantile expansion and the activities of "masculine violence" are conjoined—as a kind of discursive center from which the whole constellation of images and issues associated with empire emanates.

Roxana is a far cry from Hampton Court, or maybe not so far. Certainly Defoe's novel is socially and generically very distant from Pope's aristocratic and neoclassical poem; *Roxana* comes close to a popular tradition and views issues of class status from the opposite end of the hierarchy that *The Rape of the Lock* casually affirms. What does the very different cultural context of Defoe's *Roxana* add to this particular account of the representation of women in eighteenth-century literary culture? First and most obvious is the novel's pervasive engagement with the figures and problems connected with female adornment and dress. The centerpiece of this engagement is Roxana's Turkish costume, which seems to have a mystical power of its own to attract men and women alike. In the process of her self-merchandising, Roxana repeatedly identifies with the mate-

14. Daniel Defoe, *Review* no. 43 (8 January 1713), vol. 1 (i.e. 9), in *Defoe's Review, Reproduced from the Original Editions*, intro. by Arthur Wellesley Secord (New York: Columbia University Press, 1938), facs. bk. 22, p. 85.

rial stuff in which she is dressed, resolving her problems
through changes of clothes, and defining her success by
what she is enabled to wear. She describes a gift of three
gorgeous suits of clothes and a necklace of diamonds from
the French Prince as a kind of proof of her unique ability
to prosper and succeed;[15] with great delight she disguises
herself as a Quaker—a form of moral legitimation by dress
—to avoid her old acquaintances and begin a new life; and
indeed she names herself (and her narrative) after her infa-
mous Turkish dress. The discursive premise of the narrative too, and in particular the moral ambivalence of its
treatment of Roxana's glamorous and lucrative career, is
entangled with the issue of dressing. The preface to *Roxana*
claims that if the history that follows is not as beautiful as
Roxana is, as diverting as the reader wishes, and if it is not
ultimately instructive, this must be the fault of the "Relator
. . . dressing up the Story in worse Cloaths than the *Lady*,
whose Words he speaks, prepar'd it for the World" (1). Ev-
erything in this narrative is dressed, including any claims to
moral improvement, but it is Roxana's dressing that directs
all others.

At the height of her career, Roxana's preferred form of
adornment—the Turkish dress—both enables her to market herself in the most lucrative context, and itself evokes
the spoils of an expansionist culture. It was, she says:

> the Habit of *a Turkish Princess*; the Habit I got at *Leghorn*,
> when my *Foreign prince* bought me a *Turkish* Slave, . . . the
> *Malthese* Man of War had, it seems, taken a *Turkish* Vessel
> going from *Constantinople* to *Alexandria*, in which were some
> ladies bound for *Grand Cairo* in *Egypt*; and as the Ladies were
> made Slaves, so their fine Cloaths were thus expos'd; and

15. Daniel Defoe, *Roxana*, ed. Jane Jack (Oxford: Oxford University
Press, 1981), 70–73. Subsequent references will be to this edition.

with this *Turkish* Slave, I bought the rich Cloaths too. (173–74)

The dress is the counterpart of the slave, and in this passage indistinguishable from her, and both are made available through the agency of imperialist aggression, here the unofficial imperialist rivalry of piracy. Indeed, the outfitting of the English female body in the complete and gorgeous costume of an exotic and exploited other is one dimension of the powerful motif of female dressing that characterizes eighteenth-century imperialist ideology. In *Oroonoko*, as we have seen, Behn's protagonist acquires a similar costume, and Belinda's toilet scene suggests another occasion in which the woman is attired in the materials of an exotic world. These dresses call up the more generalized cultural obsession with the connection of female adornment and trade, a connection that we have already detailed from the colonial perspective of Aphra Behn and from the aesthetic one of Alexander Pope, but they add to that connection a dimension of exotic distance and cultural or racial difference.

Defoe's representation of Roxana hangs poised on the same paradox of nature and ornament that we traced from aesthetics to empire in Pope's female figures. Even when Roxana repudiates art, her claim to complete naturalness only serves to confirm her inevitable participation in art. The French Prince hesitates to touch her face, assuming she is painted, and receives a different sort of lesson in vanity:

as he saw the Tears drop down my Cheek, he pulls out a fine Cambrick Handkerchief, and was going to wipe the Tears off, but check'd his Hand . . . I took the Hint immediately, and with a kind of pleasant Disdain, *How, my Lord!* said I, *Have you kiss'd me so often, and don't you know whether I am*

Painted, or not? Pray let your Highness satisfie yourself, that you have no Cheats put upon you; for once let me be vain enough to say, I have not deceiv'd you with false Colours: With this, I put a Handkerchief into his Hand, and taking his Hand into mine, I made him wipe my Face so hard, that he was unwilling to do it, for fear of hurting me. (72)

She next dramatically washes her face before him with hot water: "This was, indeed, more than Satisfaction, that is to say, than Believing; for it was an undeniable Demonstration, and he kiss'd my Cheeks and Breasts a thousand times, with Expressions of the greatest Surprize imaginable" (72–73). The immediate consequence of this performance is the Prince's gift of "a fine Necklace of Diamonds"—an equivalent to the "costly string of pearl" that decorates Jane Shore at the end of that play—which the Prince accounts for as a form of necessary completion: "I love, Child, *says he*, to see every thing suitable; a fine Gown and Petticoat; a fine lac'd Head; a fine Face and Neck, and no Necklace, would not have made the Object perfect" (73). Despite the purported preference for an unpainted face, this passage locates "perfection" in the adornment, not the undressed original. Between the necklace and the face, between the dress and the female body that wears it, adornment and natural beauty are in effect inseparable. This ambiguity echoes that in *The Rape of the Lock*, in which Belinda represents both unadorned beauty and the same fully adorned "perfection" preferred by Roxana's Prince. And as in *Roxana* the artfulness that confers that perfection is paradoxically both repudiated and affirmed. Like Roxana, Belinda need not be painted or even dressed at all to embody the necessary involvement of commodification with the representation of women. In both cases, even when it is unadorned or undressed, the female body itself incarnates a central cultural engagement with accumulation and expansion. As an object of commodification, then, Roxana is enlisted in the service of imperialist ideology, to mystify its most aggressive forces.

But Roxana's implication in mercantile capitalism has another, related, and higher stage. Through her investment of the profits from her alliances with the jeweler and the prince, she becomes, in her own words, "from a Lady of Pleasure, a Woman of Business, and of great Business too . . . . by managing my Business thus myself, and having large Sums to do with, I became as expert in it, as any She-Merchant of them all" (171, 131). She learns her business in Holland, which in this period was for English advocates of trade the national exemplar of successful management.[16] And indeed at this stage in her career she represents Defoe's ideal merchant—venturesome, independent, rapacious, and validated by her own economic success.

So vital and absorbing is this activity of progressive accumulation that it supersedes any effective representation of sexual energy. As a courtesan or a prostitute Roxana negotiates a series of sexual relationships with various male partners, but none of these engagements is figured in sexual terms, either through a representation of the female body, an allusion to sexual desire, or a pause or focal moment in the narrative process. Early in the novel, in a scene with her first lover, the landlord, Roxana provokes and witnesses an exchange that might be expected to raise issues of sexual perversity or competition, voyeurism or sadism. She puts her loyal servant Amy to bed with the landlord, deliberately instigating what might have been a crisis of conflicted sexual interest. Instead, the whole business is concluded in a few short paragraphs. First Roxana undresses Amy: "I fairly stript her, and then I threw open the Bed, and thrust

16. See James Thompson, "Dryden's *Conquest of Granada* and the Dutch Wars," *The Eighteenth Century: Theory and Interpretation* 31 (1990): 218.

her in." Roxana avows that "this is enough to convince any-
body that I did not think him my Husband"; Amy gives up
any resistance and "let[s] him do what he wou'd with her"
(46–47); Roxana stands by and watches them, but recounts
nothing she sees; and the affair is concluded with a para-
graph of recriminations from Amy, one page describing
their provision for the child she bears, and their happy return to the status quo. Here and indeed throughout the
novel, the focus of narrative investment is in the enactment
of self-interest. Roxana produces this scheme in order to
confirm her pragmatic detachment from the landlord, a
detachment that is the norm for Roxana's relationships
with all the men in the novel, including the Dutch merchant, whom she eventually marries.

In the place of the sexualized female body, this narrative
locates sensuousness in a series of visions of commodities
and of processes of acquisition: in the rich dresses of the
Prince, the tangible wealth of the jeweler, and the intensely
considered decisions and calculations by which Roxana ad-
vances in her accumulation of wealth. Roxana's progress
toward independence and even agency, as a successful
entrepreneur, might help to explain the absence of a representation of sexuality in this text, as opposed to the persistent digressions toward and direct evocations of female
sexuality that we have seen in the she-tragedy and in the
aesthetic writing of the period. As an object of commodification, the female figure seems to be readily objectified,
also, in terms of sexual difference. But as an agent of exploitation—even though her currency is her own sexuality
—Roxana, like the successful male merchant, stands outside the realm of objectification. She makes her own identity through her powers of acquisition.

Indeed, it is as a direct result of her engagement in trade
that Roxana comes to call herself a "*Man-Woman*," and that
she is explicitly named as an "Amazon" (171) by Sir Robert

Clayton (the only historical personage in the novel). In this context, Roxana rejects any form of subordination to men, in particular matrimony. She says:

> I told him [Sir Robert Clayton], I knew no State of Matrimony, but what was, at best, a State of Inferiority, if not of Bondage; that I had no Notion of it; that I liv'd a Life of absolute Liberty now; was free as I was born, and having a plentiful Fortune, I did not understand what coherence the Words *Honour* and *Obey* had with the Liberty of a *Free Woman*; that I knew no Reason Men had to engross the whole Liberty of the Race, and make the women, notwithstanding any disparity of Fortune, be subject to the Laws of Marriage, of their own making; that it was my Misfortune to be a woman, but I was resolv'd it shou'd not be made worse by the Sex; and seeing Liberty seem'd to be the Men's property, I wou'd be a *Man-Woman*; for as I was born free, I wou'd die so. (170–71)

Roxana's elevation to the status of "she-merchant" coincides with an extended attack on marriage, of which this short passage is only a closing summary. She argues at length on the topic with the Dutch Merchant, who seeks to persuade her to marry him. The definition of female liberty that emerges from this discussion originates in a concern with financial control—she says: "tho' I cou'd give up my Virtue . . . yet I wou'd not give up my Money" (147)—and it ends in a radical assertion of sexual egalitarianism:

> I return'd, that while a Woman was single, she was a Masculine in her politick Capacity; that she had then the full Command of what she had, and the full Direction of what she did; that she was a Man in her separated Capacity, to all Intents and Purposes that a Man cou'd be so to himself . . . it was my Opinion, a woman was as fit to govern and enjoy her own Estate, without a Man, as a Man was, without a woman;

and that, if she had a-mind to gratifie herself as to Sexes, she might entertain a Man, as a Man does a Mistress. (148–49)

It is no surprise that *Roxana* has been seen as a protofeminist work, and for good reason.[17] At this, her most "feminist" moment, Roxana is also closest to Defoe's ideal of mercantile success; in claiming female liberty she maintains her right to control and increase her own profits. Indeed, Defoe connected liberty quite directly with a prosperous trade: he says in the *Review*, "among all the Advantages this Nation enjoys from Liberty, the Liberty of Trade is none the least, nor has it been any of the least Occasions of the growing Wealth of this Nation."[18] For Defoe, the right to free trade was essential to national prosperity; and trade itself was the ideal result of the cooperation of Providence and Nature, dispensing mutual benefit over a variety of different customs and cultures, producing different species of things, and enabling nations of different climates and geographies to profit from each other's bounty. Money is the necessary medium of this utopic process, and the accumulation of goods is the signal of its proper functioning: "Money, where there is a Genius inspires the Mind, and gives pleasing Representations of an encrease of Gain, and especially where Wealth is gotten by Trade, it pushes on the Mind for more Trade."[19] But what is the status of a

17. For example, Shirlene Mason, *Daniel Defoe and the Status of Women* (St. Albans, Vt., and Montreal: Eden Press, 1978); Katherine Rogers, "The Feminism of Daniel Defoe," in *Women in the Eighteenth Century and Other Essays*, ed. Paul Fritz and Richard Morton (Toronto: Hakkert, 1976), 3–24; Sudesh Vaid, *The Divided Mind: Studies in Defoe and Richardson* (New Delhi: Associated Publishing House, 1979); Paula Backscheider, "Defoe's Women: Snares and Prey," *Studies in Eighteenth-Century Culture* 5 (1976): 103–20.

18. Defoe, *Review* no. 107 (2 December 1705), vol. 5, facs. bk. 13, pp. 425–26.

19. Defoe, *A General History of Discoveries and Improvements in Useful Arts*

feminism derived from a passionate advocacy of mercantile capitalism, for Defoe or for us? And where does this Amazonian image lead?

It leads to a supererogatory, Juvenalian violence. As an Amazon, Roxana figures violence, and violence materializes at the end of the novel in the cold-blooded murder of her daughter by Amy, Roxana's surrogate and a successful "Woman of Business" in her own right (245). In a sense, the Amazon trope is simply following its scheduled trajectory. But the specific shape it receives from Defoe's narrative illuminates its function in eighteenth-century literary culture. Here, feminism results in the most unwomanly form of violence—the murder of a child. In other words, the logical conclusion of the extension of the ideal of mercantile capitalist profit to women is a brutal and uncontrollable violence, a violation of the supposedly natural and benevolent forces of trade. But trade itself has produced this Amazonian feminism. Through its evocation of the feminist Amazon, this text brings trade and violence into a symptomatically significant proximity. *Roxana*, like *The Rape of the Lock* and Juvenal's sixth satire, portrays an aggressively expansionist culture but omits any account of the "masculine violence" at its base. It is women who are made to take primary responsibility for the violence in these works, even when the men in them are rapists, adulterers, or even gladiators. For Juvenal, the peace of the Roman empire was sustained by an institutionalized masculine violence, by a constant military presence at the periphery of the Roman world—in Britain, Africa, Arabia, and Egypt, and on the Danube, the Rhine, and the Euphrates. In the sixth satire, this continuous masculine violence is never

(London, 1726–27), 92. See also Defoe's *Review* no. 43 (8 January 1713), vol. 1 (i.e. 9), facs. bk. 22, pp. 85–86 and no. 54 (3 February 1713), vol. 1 (i.e. 9), facs. bk. 22, pp. 107–8.

mentioned: the "Victorious Arms" of Roman imperialism find a perverse proxy in the representation of the "women who thrive on masculine violence": "'Tis Arms and Blood and Cruelty they love." For Defoe, of course, the prosperity of the first age of English maritime imperialism was sustained by the slave trade, the colonization of the West Indies and North America, the wars against the Native Americans, and the early colonial ventures in Africa and India. In *Roxana*, the explosion of aggressive energy and exploitation that characterized this early phase of mercantile capitalist adventurism emerges in the threatening figure of the "man-woman." In the image of the Amazon, then, we can catch sight of the violence that sustains empire, and we can see through the paired myths of peace and humanism that justify imperialist ideology.

The fully elaborated development of the Amazon motif in Defoe's novel produces a constellation of ideological contradictions, in which profit and murder, violence and empire, commodification and trade, all joined with a proto-feminist female autonomy, are variously and reciprocally superimposed. One part of this process, as we have seen, connects empire and violence. The Amazon secretly serves as a proxy for the imperialist, but ultimately her private and local murder exposes his public and official violence. In the same way, commodification and trade are brought into uncomfortable proximity. The figure of the commodified woman as scapegoat for mercantile capitalist accumulation masks the male acquisitiveness that fuels the energies of imperialism, but Roxana's metamorphosis from fetishized object to merchant with profits of her own makes that mask irrelevant. The she-merchant is no longer just a proxy, but an object of fetishization and an agent of exploitation at once, and this connection makes the alienating implications of accumulation and consumption the responsibility of the merchant and the product of mercantile capitalism. Through all these symptomatic contradictions, the category of female autonomy functions as the catalyst and in the process holds its own rendezvous with violence and receives its own repudiation.

In this sense, then, the perceived threat of female liberty betrays the historical alienation and brutality of the first age of English imperialism. The female mercantile profiteer is shown to be nothing better than a murderess, and then stripped of her profits and reduced by "a dreadful Course of Calamities" to "the very Reverse of [her] former Good Days" (329–30). It should be no surprise that this vehement repudiation of female liberty also makes a woman its victim: Roxana is responsible for the murder of a daughter, not a son. The text's turn against the female mercantilist is also a turn toward a general misogyny.

This conjunction of the Amazon with the representation of mercantile capitalist ideology suggests one way of understanding the function of misogynist writing in this period. The attack on women that concludes Defoe's narrative can be referred, as we have seen, to a systematic, unacknowledged connection between women and empire. The same connection can at least partly explain the misogyny implicit in *The Rape of the Lock* and, as we shall see in Chapter 6, the systematic attacks on women in Swift's poetry and in *Gulliver's Travels*. Indeed, the attribution of commodification and violence to the female figure is the most common topic of misogynist literature in the eighteenth century. The idealization of the woman as a repository of cultural value and meaning can also be linked to the same conjuncture, for such an idealization also arises from an implicit association of women with the acquisitive, progressivist, and civilizing enterprises of an expansionist culture. But in the early eighteenth century, at a time of comparative ideological consensus in England, when the benefits of empire were rarely disputed, it is in misogynist literature that the disturbing and disruptive effects of mercantile capitalism are felt. Perhaps this unacknowledged connection with the most significant and unresolvable problems of the age begins to explain the extraordinary, seemingly supererogatory violence of eighteenth-century satires on women. We might even argue—to take this point one step too far—that misogyny can find a perverse justification in its connection with imperialism, that the great misogynist statements of the eighteenth century stand in the place of an explicit critique of empire. We will take up this political dilemma more directly in our reading of Swift. Certainly, in Defoe's case, the unwitting critique of mercantile capitalist accumulation in *Roxana* seems to be generated by the misogynist turn of the narrative from female liberty to murder. Roxana's fall, however, does not exhaust the topic of the fighting female.

Prominent among the tropes that constructed the European understanding of racial difference in the long process of exploration, discovery, and exploitation that characterizes the extension of Western European culture over the globe from the Renaissance to the modern period is the recurrent mention of a race of Amazons. The travel literature of this period is full of such accounts. Columbus in his journals reports the discovery of warlike women with stores of gold or copper in the West Indies; narratives of Cortez's travels reproduce descriptions of wealthy Amazons in Mexico. Amazons with vast supplies of gold and silver were supposed to be found in the present day Caribbean, Central America, Colombia, Peru, Chile, and the Amazon basin.[20] Among the accounts retailed in one of the most widely cir-

20. Alison Dale Taufer, "From Amazon Queen to Female Knight: The Development of the Woman Warrior in the Amadis Cycle" (Ph.D. diss., UCLA, 1988), 38–47.

culated compendia of travel narratives of the time, *Purchas His Pilgrimes*, Amazons were described in Brazil and in the region of the Amazon river.[21] Walter Raleigh gives an account of Amazons he claims to document in Guyana:

> The nations of these women are on the South side of the river in the provinces of Topago, and their chiefest strengths and retracts are in the Islands situate on the South side of the entrance some 60 leagues within the mouth of the sayd river. The memories of the like women are very ancient as well in Africa as in Asia . . . in many histories they are verified to have bene, and in divers ages and provinces: but they which are not far from Guiana Doe accompany with men but once in a yere . . . . If they conceive, and be delivered of a sonne, they returne him to the father; if of a daughter they nourish it, and reteine it . . . . It was farther told me, that if in these warres they tooke any prisoners that they used to accompany with those also at what time soever, but in the end of certeine they put them to death: for they are sayd to be very cruell and bloodthirsty, especially to such as offer to invade their territories. These Amazones have likewise great store of these plates of gold.[22]

Various travelers place Amazons in parts of Africa, especially Ethiopia. Father Francisco Alvarez describes a race of

---

21. See "The Admirable adventures and strange fortunes of Master Anthonie Knivet . . . 1591" and "A Description and Discoverie of the River of Amazons, by William Davies Barber Surgeon of London," in Samuel Purchas, *Hakluytus Posthumus; or, Purchas His Pilgrimes* (London, 1616; reprint, 20 vols., Glasgow: James MacLehose, 1906), 16:177–289 and 16:413–16.

22. "The discoverie of the large, rich, and beautifull Empire of Guiana . . . by Sir Walter Ralegh," in Richard Hakluyt, *The Principal Navigations Voyages Traffiques and Discoveries of the English Nation* (London, 1589; reprint, 12 vols., Glasgow: James MacLehose, 1904), 10:366–67. Louis Montrose provides an account of the role of the Amazon myth in Renaissance culture, and of Raleigh's "ethnography of the Amazons" in particular ("The Work of Gender in the Discourse of Discovery," *Representations* 33 [1991]: esp. 26–27).

warlike women in Ethiopia, a "kingdom of the Amazons":
"I was . . . assured, that on the Frontiers . . . , as you travell
toward the South there is a Kingdome governed by women,
which may be called Amazones . . . . they have no King but
a Queene that hath no certaine Husband, but suffereth any
man to lye with her, and to get her with child, and the
eldest Daughter succeedeth in the Kingdome." According
to this account, "They gather great store of Gold in this
Kingdome" and their supplies serve as the source of the
gold that is thence exported to other parts of Africa.[23] And
elsewhere in *Purchas* we can find similar stories of African
Amazons: in the report of Pigafetta's travels there is an empire in the Congo called Monomotapa, whose prize warriors are female legions: "These Women doe burne their
left paps with fire, because they should be no hindrance
unto them in their shooting, after the use and manner of
the ancient Amazons." They too keep only their female
children.[24] And also in *Purchas* Bermudez, another traveler
to Ethiopia, has heard of Amazons there as well: "neere
to Damute, [there is] a Province of women without men:
which doe live after the manner of the ancient Amazones
of Scythia."[25]

Throughout this period Amazons are purportedly sighted
just beyond the limits of European geographical penetra-
tion, and they are frequently described as possessing the
very precious metals that inspired those early dreams of
exploitation. These Amazons are always warlike races, typically accomplished and bloodthirsty fighters who are often

23. "The Voyage of Sir Francis Alvarez, a Portugall Priest, made into
. . . Ethiopia, *Continued*," in Purchas, *Purchas His Pilgrimes*, 7:205–6. See
also Taufer, "From Amazon Queen to Female Knight," 36.
24. "A report of the Kingdome of Congo, a Region of Affrica, gathered
by Philippo Pigafetta, out of the Discourses of Master Edward Lopes a
Portugell," in Purchas, *Purchas His Pilgrimes*, 6:508.
25. "A Brief Relation . . . which . . . John Bermudez brought from . . .
Ethiopia," in Purchas, *Purchas His Pilgrimes*, 7:363.

said to amputate or cauterize a breast in order better to use the bow. Their sexual arrangements are a common source of comment; they are sometimes said to have intercourse with male prisoners of war or at infrequent, prearranged times with neighboring tribes. By some reports, they return any male children to their fathers, and sometimes they are said to murder male offspring, a form of programmatic violence that is taken as another emblem of their unnatural brutality.

Raleigh and others allude to a venerable tradition that shapes these "discoveries" of warlike women: "the memories of [Amazons] *are* very ancient" [my italics] in Western European culture. In classical discourse Amazons serve as a figure for the uncivilized races beyond the boundaries of the known world—in Libya, Ethiopia, and Central Asia— and for the threat of barbarian invasion posed by those alien peoples. In the medieval period the story of an Amazon society embodied an inversion of Western European social and cultural structures and thus defined the limits of social stability, and again this alien society is typically located in Ethiopia or in India. In representing their encounter with the worlds beyond Europe, their confrontation with the disorienting experience of geographical and racial otherness, the Renaissance chroniclers availed themselves of a version of the figure that had represented racial difference for over two millennia, locating and shaping that ideologically efficacious figure according to the new requirements of Western European imperialism.

We have here a rather stark logical contradiction. The Amazon of one pervasive contemporary discourse is a figure for the native; but in another powerful canonical and popular construct, the Amazon is the alter ego of the male European imperialist. Finding this figure on both sides of the imperialist coin suggests that the Amazon functions as a strong common denominator in mercantile capitalist ideology: a common denominator for difference. I think our reading so far of the use of the Amazon in the representation of women in the early eighteenth century has given us the right to speculate a bit on the components of that common denominator. The woman and the native can be seen as equivalent categories in the construction of difference: both represent objects to be controlled, manipulated, and exploited, economically as well as sexually, and thus they fall together under the same figure. But also, both the female other and the native other evoke a complex social, political, and sexual threat, a threat compactly realized in and constituted by the Amazon image. Roxana, as we have seen, comes to control the profits accruing from the exploitation of her body, and so moves from an object of commodification to an agent of trade. And natives, too, might be seen as potential agents in their own context. To the extent that they are viewed as possessing their own land and property, especially gold and other precious metals, they might move from exploited object to threatening agent in their own right. As Raleigh says, "they are . . . very cruell and bloodthirsty, especially to such as offer to invade their territories." That is, the category of difference in this period embraces doubly both object and agent, exploitation and resistance. We can approach the structure of this ambiguity through a reading of the representation of the African and of the relation between difference and trade in Defoe's *Captain Singleton*.

This diffuse novel falls into roughly two parts. The first, initiated by a mutiny, describes the travels of a small group of European sailors across the African continent from present-day Mozambique to Guinea (or West Africa), their encounters with the natives, and their discovery, mining, and accumulation of gold. By Singleton's account, the European adventurers are the first human beings in the African landscape. The narrative repeatedly asserts that "Never

Man, nor a Body of Men" crossed the desert they encountered before they did; "no human Hands" fished in the
great lake they find in their way.[26] These Eurocentric assertions of discovery directly contradict the narrative's simultaneous accounts of the populousness of the country. The
Africans are ubiquitous and significant in the novel. In contrast to the countryside, which is represented as "very
pleasant and fruitful, and a convenient Place enough to live
in," the Africans are typically described as "a Parcel of
Creatures scarce human, or capable of being made sociable
on any Account whatsoever" (21). Because they are not
seen as human, their difference, racial or otherwise, from
the European adventurers is at first barely recognized; they
form a part of the landscape like the trees, rivers, and hills
(73). Though they are heard to speak, they seem to have no
intelligible language (48); their speech is confused with animal noises (81, 107); and if they can be made to communi-
cate, they use only signs (82). The Africans whom the travelers manage to domesticate and who travel with them as
guides and cargo-bearers occupy two categories. Either
they are Europeanized—like the Black Prince, an Oro-
onoko-like character endowed with a chivalric notion of
honor and heroic accomplishments to match—or they are
the crucial figures in maximizing gold accumulation; they
point it out to the travelers variously throughout their journey and perform the labor essential to its extraction.

The centrality of gold in the African section of *Captain
Singleton* is a significant anachronism. At the time of the
novel's writing—in 1720—and also at the time of its setting—about twenty years earlier—gold was much less significant than slaves in the African trade. In this novel and

26. Daniel Defoe, *Captain Singleton*, ed. Shiv K. Kumar (Oxford: Oxford University Press, 1973), 86–87. Subsequent references to this work
will be to this edition.

in his numerous periodical essays on the Royal African
Company (between 1709 and 1713), Defoe writes almost
exclusively about the accumulation of gold.[27] Slavery is an
occasional matter, subsidiary often to the discovery and extraction of the African gold. This anachronism need not
suggest that slavery was a problematic issue for Defoe; but
the focus on gold does seem to indicate that primitive accumulation and its logical extension into trade occupies a crucial position in the text. It is significant that the question of
the subjectivity of the natives arises mainly in relation to
precious metals. That is, the point at which the Africans
briefly acquire human status—albeit of a negative sort—
occurs in their relationship to these vast supplies of gold
with which they are surrounded. They are considered fools
for not knowing its worth; and fools are considered human. Even though the explorers acknowledge that gold is
of no use without trade (127), and even though the acquisitiveness it inspires is also occasionally associated with Satan
through the kind of anachronistic moralism typical in Defoe's writings (131), each time the Africans innocently direct the travelers to deposits of gold which they show no
interest in possessing themselves, or choose some more useful metal over golden ornaments (93, 107), they are made
to seem strikingly defective in discernment. On these occasions, they are treated not as trees or beasts, but as human
beings basically comparable, if radically inferior, to the Europeans. The implicit assumption of the narrative at these
points is that trade defines civilization; and that an understanding of exchange value is inherently superior to a dependence on use value. Civilization and racial superiority
are thus associated with exchange value. Trade and money
are the catalysts here, producing in the context of an asser-

27. See Samuel Kwaku Opoku, "The Image of Africa, 1660–1730 (Defoe and Travel Literature)," (Ph.D. diss., Princeton University, 1967), 4.

tion of racial superiority the text's only acknowledgment of racial difference. We might say that trade, or the potential for trade, transforms the natives from trees or beasts into human others—just as the association with trade transforms Roxana from an object of commodification to a figure of female autonomy.

The African section of *Captain Singleton* is succeeded by a long account of Singleton's exploits as a pirate. This account of piracy, just like the African travels of the first section, focuses on the accumulation of riches. Both represent the aspiration to subject the world to capitalist exchange. Like the travelers of the first half, the pirates are single-mindedly devoted to the pursuit of profit; so much so that the narrative of their exploits and adventures is notably tame, focusing exclusively upon the goods and riches they accumulate. It seems appropriate that most of the wealth they carry off is the intercepted product of imperial trade with what we would now call the third world. In short, *Captain Singleton*'s piracy—"the Plunder of so many innocent . . . Nations"(266)—is another redaction of European mercantile capitalism and a version of the common contemporary process, in this period of early capitalist development, by which an apparently erratic and private form of exploitation becomes a legitimate and official dimension of imperialist expansion.[28] Indeed, *Singleton*'s pirates are inter-

28. In "Dryden's *Conquest of Granada*," James Thompson provides a useful definition of this phenomenon: "The Dutch wars were fought over trade, and they should be seen as an official extension or a systematic venture above and beyond ordinary competition and the normal preying upon shipping and one another's outposts in the East and West Indies and along the West African coast. An analogy can be drawn here between the last phase of enclosure, as E. P. Thompson presents it in *Whigs and Hunters, the Origins of the Black Act*, and the struggle over navigation, maritime law, and fishing rights—the official pretexts for the Dutch wars . . . ; in both cases, what we see is a bourgeois process of systematizing exploitation by legitimating it. The same process is at work in the struggle over the

changeable with traders. The Quaker William serves as the linking figure between piracy and trade. He acts as the pirates' trading agent on more than one occasion (250), and he makes it clear that money is the real goal of their enterprise:

> Why, says *William* gravely, I only ask what is thy Business, and the Business of all the people thou hast with thee? Is it not to get Money? Yes, *William*, it is so, in our honest Way: And wouldst thou, says he, rather have Money without Fighting, or Fighting without Money? O *William, says I*, the first of the two, to be sure. (153–54)

From this perspective, he can argue against attacks on some unruly natives at Java, explaining "your Business is Money" (219) rather than vengeance. And he can, when profit calls, trade in slaves (164) despite his sympathy for the Negroes taken in a slave ship earlier in the narrative (157, 160). Thus William functions as an exemplar of capitalist ideology, programmatically subordinating morality to profit and ingeniously increasing the pirates' profit at every turn. He merges unobtrusively with the pirates, or emerges unobtrusively from them, first claiming he is made a pirate by force, then claiming he is a pacifist (144, 212), but swiftly making their work his own. The pirates, like Roxana, are protected morally by association with the Quaker, and this trick helps to turn aside criticism of the image of rapacious accumulation. William, then, functions as one of the means by which the ideology of capitalist expansion systematically obscures its necessary racism, violence, and exploitation through claims of egalitarianism and benevolence.

But just as this superimposition of piracy and trade makes the pirates traders, it makes all traders pirates. That is, it

---

use of privateers and pirates: colonization is the legitimating and the systematizing of a formerly episodic rapine" (218).

connects an illicit form of violence with the supposedly benevolent official processes of capitalist accumulation. Like
Roxana, then, *Captain Singleton* systematically converts its
protagonist's primary activity into trade, and in the process
functions to reveal the necessary violence of imperialist ideology. Trade is the common denominator of the two parts
of *Captain Singleton*, integrating the acquisition of gold (in
Africa) and goods (through piracy) as joint dimensions of
the urgent enterprise of primary accumulation. And again
as in *Roxana*, the association of trade and violence governs
the unconscious structure of the novel. For both narratives,
the figure of difference is constituted through this treatment of trade. The Africans become significantly other
only through reference to their gold, just as Roxana becomes an Amazon through becoming a merchant, which is
accordingly and paradoxically the source of her otherness.
Ironically, the more a male, mercantile sensibility is attributed to Roxana, the more threatening and different she
becomes. And the natives in *Captain Singleton* become more
different the closer they approach the capitalist concept of
trade and exchange. That is, the difference both of the native Amazon and of the female Amazon is a product of
their proximity to imperialist accumulation. In this sense,
Roxana evokes the other within, the disruptive power of a
category of difference internal to the dominant ideology.
And *Captain Singleton* reveals the other without, measuring
and taming difference with the European yardstick and
bludgeon of accumulation.

Under the sign of difference, the Amazon illuminates a
whole constellation of ideological categories and functions.
As a proxy or scapegoat, the representation of difference
serves discursively to deflect the responsibilities and anxieties of empire. That process of deflection itself—by which
the other takes on the powers of the merchant or the po-

tential to engage in exchange—functions to demystify imperialist ideology. Dressed thus by deflection in the guise of
power, the Amazon briefly serves to formulate a discourse
of radical difference, a feminist reading of the bourgeois
category of liberty. The repudiation of that radical critique
is in turn a catalyst for the demystification of imperialist
ideology. Finally, as a figure for the other, the image of the
Amazon includes and thus conjoins both women and natives. This conjunction is founded on the discursive proximity of difference and trade, and that proximity in turn
serves as the prerequisite for the various odd configura-
tions in the dramatization of imperialist ideology that this
reading of the figure of the Amazon has enabled us to observe.

I raised two issues at the outset of this chapter. The first
was a specific question: does the fact that we have viewed
the Amazon through the discourse of the dominant ideology make any account of resistance or subversion of that
ideology inaccessible to us? If we generalize from this question, we arrive first at the other issue to which I promised
to return. That is, if we ask abstractly: how does this argument figure as a form of radical political criticism, we can
begin to propose a political purpose for recent "political"
readings.

One purpose of this particular reading resides in part in
the recovery and re-presentation of a critical position relevant to a progressive politics—the argument for female liberty. Deriving the advocacy of women's liberty from the
advocacy of exploitation seems to violate the supposedly
egalitarian assumptions of a liberationist critique. And of
course in the case of *Roxana* any advocacy of female autonomy we might derive is even further qualified by the
novel's ultimate repudiation of Roxana's protofeminism. In
other words, what is the use of a feminism that comes out
of imperialism and that is so vehemently disowned by its

author? It can open up the argument for bourgeois liberty upon which much modern feminism depends; it can show us that the female liberty defined by Roxana is the logical extension of the bourgeois ideal of a universalist humanism that underlies the notion of free enterprise and economic individualism. And it can illuminate the radical potential of that ideal just as it provides a cautionary indication of its limitations. This problematic feminism thus enables us to engage the important and politically useful question of whether and to what extent the argument for female liberty can be disentangled from capitalist ideology.

Such a reading can also be used symptomatically, as political demystification rather than recovery. We have seen through this account of the Amazon how ideology functions to incorporate or subsume categories of difference and turn them to its own ends; how an ideology that seems hegemonic and self-justifying unwittingly produces its own negation; how the universalist perspective of a dominant ideology might be fissured or flawed. In this way, the dramatization of an ostensibly monolithic ideology can provide various forms of leverage, various sightings of alternative categories, various points of contention that displace, disorient, or disrupt that discourse. Ends like these might justify the complex process of explication through which modern essays in "political" criticism—such as this one—construct literary culture.

But there is another, more speculative possibility, which I raise in partial answer to the question of the limitation of our perspective to the view of the imperialist. Perhaps this argument indicates that even in the context of the dramatization of an oppressive ideology representations of difference cannot be suppressed. The use of the marginal as a proxy for power, although it seems a perfect act of appropriation, might trigger the potential for subversion, however ambiguously it is realized. Furthermore, the Amazon, by occupying the positions of the native other and of the female other and by functioning in both to expose the violence and self-interest concealed behind the humanist claims of imperialist ideology, might mark an instance of joint disruption, a point of articulation where a common system of oppression encounters a common resistance. This point of articulation, if we can reach it, might make the aims of "political" criticism compatible with a liberationist politics.

6

Imperial Disclosures:
Jonathan Swift

To say the truth, I had conceived a few scruples with relation
to the distributive justice of princes upon those occasions. For
instance, a crew of pirates are driven by a storm they know
not whither, at length a boy discovers land from the topmast,
they go on shore to rob and plunder, they see an harmless
people, are entertained with kindness, they give the country a
new name, they take formal possession of it for the king . . .
they murder two or three dozen of the natives . . . return
home, and get their pardon. . . . Ships are sent with the first
opportunity, the natives driven out or destroyed, their princes
tortured to discover their gold . . . and this execrable crew of
butchers employed in so pious an expedition, is a modern colony sent to convert and civilize an idolatrous and barbarous
people.

But this description, I confess, doth by no means affect the
British nation.

Jonathan Swift, *Gulliver's Travels*

I use Swift's works in this final chapter in part as a
way of coming to a conclusion, or at least an end point, on
the issue of a radical political criticism and of the truth that
such a criticism can claim. It has become increasingly evident that the notion of political criticism cannot stand
alone, either as the designation of revisionist or radical
work in the study of literary culture at large, or as the definition of a new perspective on eighteenth-century literature
in particular. After all, there is nothing new in reading

eighteenth-century literature in its historical and political contexts; of all the historical periods of English literary studies, the eighteenth century has been the most resistant to versions of formalist analysis, including New Criticism, and the most strongly grounded in an attention to politics and history. What sort of claim can a political reading make in a field already permeated by political awareness?

And more broadly speaking, the meaning of the political itself, in recent critical discourse, has been at best diffuse. Does it suggest a minimal sensitivity to topical and contextual reference—the mode most typical of eighteenth-century studies? Or does it more tendentiously denote a specific theoretical orientation or a systematic political project—like contemporary work in Marxist, feminist, and new historicist criticism, and the recent studies of race and colonialism? My position throughout this study has been based, first, on the assumption that a description of historical parallels, public themes, or topical political satires cannot serve as an adequate indication of the political significance of this literature or of the ideological structures so crucially consolidated in the literary culture of the English eighteenth century. For this reason I find it necessary to distinguish my political readings rather rigorously from traditional political criticism in eighteenth-century studies. My readings are designed to shift the political from the arena of contextual reference to that of structural and theoretical analysis. But the larger task of this study has been to give the political a politics, to sort out from the range of possible meanings of "political" a definition that fits the purposes of a radical critique of ideology and that differentiates itself from political criticism whose end does not coincide with explicitly liberationist political commitments. In this sense, I would distinguish my method, my concerns, and my conclusions not only from those of critics uninterested in such matters as gender, race, class, and empire—the large ma-

jority of my colleagues in and out of the eighteenth century—but also from those of most American new historicist
and political critics, whose historical analyses are not explicitly aimed at a liberationist project. This may seem a rather
fine distinction within a largely coherent body of contemporary criticism, but I think it only seems so until we attempt to explain the aim of our political criticism and the
ends that we expect our uses of history to serve.

In that spirit, I would like to preface this reading of
Swift's works with a rehearsal of the programmatic and
polemical assertions with which I began this book, hoping
that by now, at least for the purpose of argument, these
claims will be granted as generally plausible. First and most
broadly, let's say that eighteenth-century English literature
can only be understood in the context of the triumph and
consolidation of English imperialism, and that the functioning of imperialist ideology in this period is likewise only to
be understood in terms of the crucial role of slavery, the
economic exploitation of racial difference. Furthermore, underlying the construction of imperialist ideology, let's say, is
the fetishization of the figure of the woman as agent,
proxy, prototype, or embodiment of the effects of mercantile capitalism, and that figure provides the critic with a
special lever against the complex structure of bourgeois
thought. The human commodity and the commodified female—figures of racial and sexual difference—are thus intimately if not explicitly connected. Analysis of their mutual
interaction provides a method by which the literary culture
of this period can be understood both in its connection with
the hegemonic forces of capital and empire and in its relation to the diffuse positions of resistance variously and sep-
arately deployed but never allied against those forces.

I have tried at length in the course of this book to support these assertions: in the account of *Oroonoko* in Chapter
2 through a dialectical connection of race and gender mediated by the female figure, which reveals an implicit mutu-

ality between the woman and the slave in their relationship to colonialist culture; in Chapter 5 through an account of the Amazon as a common denominator of difference that, in the discursive proximity of trade, includes and thus conjoins both women and natives; and in Chapters 3 and 4 through a pair of sustained readings of the sexualized and fetishized figure of the woman and her relation to mercantile capitalism. In this chapter I will pursue the engagement with colonialism and the claim of the mutual interaction of race and gender in the context of the writings of an explicit misogynist who is also an explicit anticolonialist in order to test once more this methodological and political thesis. Jonathan Swift is the eighteenth-century writer who has been perhaps most widely and continuously subject to political criticism, from the first publication of the *Tale of a Tub* to the present. In this respect, he serves as an index of the durability of the political in discussions of literary culture but also, in my immediate context, as a proving ground for an account of the various, potentially incompatible purposes of political readings. Swift's texts show us the difference, in both method and aim, between political criticism in general and a radical or Marxist critique in particular, by providing an occasion for a dialectical reading of the relation between gender and race, and by raising the question of the place of a liberationist politics in an account of literary culture. My general aim in this concluding chapter, then, is to demonstrate the mutual interaction of issues of gender and race in Swift's major satire, and thus to uncover the necessary connection between the positions of the oppressed at that stage in the history of English capitalism associated broadly with commodity exchange and colonial expansion.

This connection will return us at the end of my argument to the aim of the political, to the crucial task of distinguishing among political readings by their implicit political uses. In Swift's case, as we shall see, the implications of a

critique from the perspective of gender, which must view
Swift in the context of the brutal and violent tradition of
misogynist satire, would seem to aim at a political assessment diametrically opposed to that suggested by a critique
from the perspective of race or colonialism, which would
number Swift, the Irish nationalist, among the earliest and
most explicit and consistent critics of imperialism of his century. In other words, Swift's texts lend themselves equally
well to a negative and a positive hermeneutic, and a critic
concerned with the political aim of her readings of literary
culture might well pause between the exposure of misogyny in the canon and the discovery of an early ally in the
struggle against colonialism. Which to choose? What is a
marxist/feminist to do? By arguing for the mutual interaction of gender and race in Swift's works, I want to use that
dilemma to provide a working example of a radical political
criticism. The paradigm provided by Swift's problematic
texts suggests the political utility of bringing positive and
negative hermeneutics together, and defines what I see to
be the necessary intimacy of structures of oppression and
liberation in early eighteenth-century culture.

From a feminist point of view, the oppression is not hard
to find, and indeed recent feminist critics have found much
of interest in Swift's writing.[1] Aside from topical political

---

1. See Felicity A. Nussbaum, *The Brink of All We Hate: English Satires on
Women, 1660–1750* (Lexington: University of Kentucky Press, 1984);
Ellen Pollak, *The Poetics of Sexual Myth: Gender and Ideology in the Verse of
Swift and Pope* (Chicago: University of Chicago Press, 1985); Penelope
Wilson, "Feminism and the Augustans: Some Readings and Problems,"
Critical Quarterly 28 (1986): 80–92; and Katherine M. Rogers, *The Trouble-
some Helpmate: A History of Misogyny in Literature* (Seattle: University of
Washington Press, 1966), and *Feminism in Eighteenth-Century England* (Ur-
bana: University of Illinois Press, 1982). The difficulty Swift presents for a
feminist reading is suggested by the fact that Rogers's first book presents
Swift as a misogynist (*Troublesome Helpmate*, 174) and her second as a feminist (*Feminism in Eighteenth-Century England*, 61), on identical evidence.

subjects, the single most significant theme in Swift's poetry is the attack on women. These misogynist poems—"The Progress of Beauty," the dressing room poems, "Strephon and Chloe," "Cassinus and Peter," and others—were written between 1719 and 1731, the decade of *Gulliver's Travels* (1726), *A Modest Proposal* (1729), *The Drapier's Letters* (1724–25), and Swift's most energetic defense of Ireland against British colonialist policies. They belong to that venerable tradition of misogynist verse, which we have seen to be associated with Juvenal, and whose contemporary exemplars include Rochester, Mandeville, and Pope. They focus on the corruption and decay of the female body through images of painting and dressing, excrement and disease.

"The Lady's Dressing Room" is typical of their structure. It begins with a description of the artifice by which the true, corrupt nature of the female body is concealed:

> Five Hours, (and who can do it less in?)
> By haughty *Celia* spent in Dressing;
> The Goddess from her chamber issues,
> Array'd in Lace, Brocades and Tissues.[2]
>
> (1–4)

When Celia leaves the scene, the poem proceeds to undress her in her absence by picking through the contents of her dressing room. And this undressing climaxes in the most memorable passage in eighteenth-century misogyny:

> Thus finishing his grand Survey,
> Disgusted *Strephon* stole away
> Repeating in his amorous Fits,
> Oh! *Celia, Celia, Celia* shits!
>
> (125–28)

2. Jonathan Swift, *The Poems of Jonathan Swift*, ed. Harold Williams (Oxford: Clarendon Press, 1937). References by line to Swift's poems will be to this edition.

The degeneration of the absent Celia ends with the mock-advice to Strephon:

> I pity wretched *Strephon* blind
> To all the Charms of Female Kind;
> Should I the Queen of Love refuse,
> Because she rose from stinking Ooze?
>
> . . . .
>
> When *Celia* in her Glory shows,
> If *Strephon* would but stop his Nose;
>
> . . . .
>
> He soon would learn to think like me,
> And bless his ravisht Sight to see
> Such Order from Confusion sprung,
> Such gaudy Tulips rais'd from Dung.
>
> (115–44)

When Gulliver stops his nose with rue to avoid the nauseous scent of his wife at the end of part 4 of *Gulliver's Travels*, he is taking the advice the poet gives to Strephon in this poem, and aspiring—though with a pointed lack of success—to the ironically liberated position of the speaker here, enacting the very extent of his disgust by claiming to accept the inevitability of an essential, gendered corruption.

Celia and the much-neglected Mrs. Gulliver are the absent objects of an attack that clearly exceeds their own poor power to offend. Though the female body is the purported locus of corruption in the misogynist poetry, it seems often to be slipping from sight, like the Celia of "The Progress of Beauty," who melts away piece by piece, a hideous victim of syphilis, so that by the end of the poem,

> When Mercury her Tresses mows
> To think of Oyl and Soot, is vain,
> No Painting can restore a Nose,

Nor will her Teeth return again.
Two Balls of Glass may serve for Eyes,
White Lead can plaister up a Cleft,
But these alas, are poor Supplyes
If neither Cheeks, nor Lips be left.

(109–16)

In fact there is no woman left at all in these attacks on women. The female body is displaced by the materials with which it is adorned, or, ultimately, shored up: from dress to paint to plaster, "Crystal Eyes," and "artificial Hair" ("A Beautiful Young Nymph," lines 10–11). What is the status of a misogyny that, while claiming to condemn an essential corruption, so quickly substitutes the accoutrements and ornaments of the female body for the woman herself? Or rather, what is the ideological status of this purported essentiality?

The representation of female adornment and dress in this period, as we well know by now, typically evokes the contemporary context of mercantile capitalist accumulation. In the account of Pope's aesthetic writings in Chapter 4, we traced the process by which the female figure is first of all associated with the products of consumption through the commodities that adorn her, and then identified in her very body with trade itself. In this process the woman is, like Swift's Celia, subsumed by the materials with which she is dressed. In Addison's description of "woman as a beautiful, romantic animal,"[3] as in Rowe's vision of Jane Shore's consumption of "foreign vintages" and "silken stores,"[4] and the numerous other contemporary images

3. Joseph Addison, *Tatler* no. 116 (5 January 1709–10), in *The Tatler*, ed. Donald F. Bond, 3 vols. (Oxford: Clarendon Press, 1987), 2:125.
4. Nicholas Rowe, *The Tragedy of Jane Shore*, V.i.111–17, in *British Dramatists from Dryden to Sheridan*, ed. George H. Nettleton and Arthur E. Case (Boston: Houghton Mifflin, 1939).

that make women the inspiration of the merchant or the destination of the products of trade, the trope of dressing naturalizes the enterprise of mercantile capitalism, so that all of nature seems to cooperate in decorating the female figure, and the notion of an acquisitive agent whose motive is self-interest and whose aim is accumulation is deferred, repressed, or deflected into an attack on female vanity or even female character. This naturalization of trade and its identification with the woman leads, as we observed in both Pope and Defoe, to a reversal of agent and object, in which the female consumer or object of adornment takes the place of the male adventurer or profiteer. This trope shapes celebratory accounts of female beauty and desirability, as well as misogynist attacks on women as the embodiment of cultural corruption, and sometimes both, as in Mandeville's account of the role of female luxury in promoting the prosperity of a capitalist economy, in which celebration and satire coincide. Mandeville, as we have seen, compares the historical significance of the petticoat to that of the Reformation partly in order to expose the "silly and capricious" habits of female consumption and partly in order to indicate the world-historical significance that he would attach to the chain of effects beginning in female consumption and issuing in a profitable trade, a prosperous economy, and an "opulent, powerful, and . . . flourishing" English imperialism.[5]

It is not surprising, in this context, to find in Swift's Irish tracts "A Proposal to the Ladies of Ireland" (1729), which suggests that the distresses of the Irish economy, caused by the colonialist trade restrictions imposed by England, can only be remedied by a restriction in turn upon "the impor-

5. Bernard Mandeville, *The Fable of the Bees: or, Private Vices, Publick Benefits*, ed. F. B. Kaye, 2 vols. (Oxford: Clarendon Press, 1924), I.356, 225–28.

tation of all unnecessary commodities," namely and specifically those for female consumption. Here Swift too takes for granted an intimate connection between female luxury and capitalism. But in this case the benefits of the accumulation of manufactured goods accrue to the English economy, not the Irish, and thus Swift draws the opposite conclusions from Mandeville:

> It is to gratify the vanity and pride, and luxury of the women . . . that we owe this unsupportable grievance of bringing in the instruments of our ruin. There is annually brought over to this kingdom near ninety thousand pounds worth of silk, whereof the greater part is manufactured: Thirty thousand pounds more is expended in muslin, holland, cambric, and callico. . . . If the ladies, till better times, will not be content to go in their own country shifts, I wish they may go in rags. Let them vie with each other in the fineness of their native linen: Their beauty and gentleness will as well appear, as if they were covered over with diamonds and brocade.[6]

Elsewhere in the Irish tracts, economic and misogynist sentiments come even more directly into synchrony:

> Is it not the highest Indignity to human nature, that men should be such poltrons as to suffer the Kingdom and themselves to be undone, by the Vanity, the Folly, the Pride, and Wantonness of their Wives, who under their present Corruptions seem to be a kind of animal suffered for our sins to be sent into the world for the Destruction of Familyes, Societyes, and Kingdoms; and whose whole study seems directed to be as expensive as they possibly can in every useless article of living, who by long practice can reconcile the most pernicious

6. Jonathan Swift, "A Proposal that All the Ladies and Women of Ireland should appear constantly in Irish Manufactures," in *Prose Works*, ed. Herbert Davis, 14 vols. (Oxford: Oxford University Press, 1951), 12:126–27.

forein Drugs to their health and pleasure, provided they are
but expensive; as Starlings grow fat with henbane: who contract a Robustness by meer practice of Sloth and Luxury: who
can play deep severall hours after midnight, sleep beyond
noon, revel upon Indian poisons, and spend the revenue of a
moderate family to adorn a nauseous unwholesom living Carcase.[7]

This passage makes the same economic assumptions about
female adornment that we have associated with mercantile
capitalist ideology, and with the same reversal of agent and
object typical of that ideology. But here the attack on female luxury concludes with an evocation of and attack on
the body of the woman, a process that reverses the movement we traced in *Jane Shore* from the female body to commodification. Easily and unobtrusively, by the end of this
passage the female body, rather than her dress, becomes
the locus of cultural corruption, and this "nauseous unwholesome living Carcase" brings us back to the revolting
female body that stands behind the representation of
women in the misogynist poetry. The reversal of cause and
effect at work here is characteristic of Swift's misogyny
throughout his writings. Through a kind of metonymy, the
products of mercantile capitalism with which women surround and adorn themselves come to be implicated with
the female body itself. That is, the pernicious corruptions
of an expansionist culture are so intimately and inevitably
associated with the figure of the woman that they are represented as intrinsic rather than extrinsic to her; the nau-
seousness of the female body is thus a visceral representation of what Mandeville, and Swift himself in the Irish
tracts, describe as an economic and social corruption. Even
when the woman is absent, melted away by the disease she

7. Swift, "Answer to Several Letters from Unknown Persons" (1729),
in *Prose Works*, 12:80.

embodies, or when she is supplanted altogether by the products that she wears, we see her body as the epitome of an essential corruption. And reciprocally, when she is present but undressed—presumably stripped of the corrupting commodity—she still appears as the essential incarnation of the evils of luxury and accumulation. Present or absent, dressed or undressed, the figure of the woman is made to take responsibility for the cultural crisis of mercantile capitalism and imperial expansion. Thus, though the position of the Irish tracts would suggest that Celia's corruption originates in the products with which she is adorned—her dress, in the misogynist poetry those products no longer appear as a cause of corruption; instead they are an innocent adjunct, an effect of Celia's essential corruption, simply absorbing the stench that arises directly from the inherent corruption of the "Female Kind":

> So Things, which must not be exprest,
> When plumpt into the reeking Chest;
> Send up an excremental Smell
> To taint the Parts from whence they fell.
> The Pettycoats and Gown perfume,
> Which waft a Stink round every Room.
>
> (524–30)

Excrement taints the female body, then her petticoat—that cultural signal of conspicuous consumption—then her dress, then "every Room" she visits, so that ultimately the world inhabited by this female figure seems to receive corruption from her rather than bestow it upon her, in a process that symptomatically inverts the movement from the consumption of luxuries to the "nauseous unwholesom living Carcase" of the Irish tracts.

If we use the Irish tracts to locate Swift's misogyny in relation to the widespread contemporary discourse of women and commodities, then, we can begin to see beneath the claim of essential female corruption that dominates the poetry the fundamental implication of Swift's misogyny with mercantile capitalism. In the poetry, this implication is unacknowledged and probably unconscious, but it supplies us with one way of understanding the seemingly super-erogatory violence of Swift's disturbing attacks on women; and one way of placing misogyny in the context of Swift's writings. In short, it enables us to provide a particular ac-count of the historical status and ideological significance of these otherwise anomalous texts. The misogynist poetry is a record of the cultural consequences of commodification, and its visceral revulsion reflects the historical crisis of this period with a vehemence and horror that is significantly absent from any explicit contemporary commentary. In other words, at a time of comparative ideological con-sensus, when the benefits of empire were rarely disputed, Swift's attacks on women occupy the place of a critique of mercantile capitalist expansion. This observation is no justi-fication for misogyny, but it complicates a political reading of Swift, and more important, it leads us to other images and other critiques of imperialism elsewhere in Swift's writ-ing.

If we bring this reading of the misogynist poetry to bear upon *Gulliver's Travels*, we can move from the ideological status of women in Swift's writing and the connection of the representation of women with capitalist expansion to the historical problem of colonialism as it shapes the most important satire of the eighteenth century, and we can be-gin to see the mutual interaction of race and gender in Swift's major satire.

Part 2 of *Gulliver's Travels* supplies the famous images of the gigantic female body that put Gulliver in precisely the

place of Strephon in "The Lady's Dressing Room" when he
picks up the magnifying mirror:

> The Virtues we must not let pass,
> Of *Celia*'s magnifying Glass.
> When frighted *Strephon* cast his Eye on't
> It shew'd the Visage of a Gyant.
> A Glass that can to Sight disclose,
> The smallest Worm in *Celia*'s Nose,
> And faithfully direct her Nail
> To squeeze it out from Head to Tail.
>
> (59–66)

Brobdingnagian gigantism is intimately linked to misogyny.
Indeed, the scenes in part 2 that focus on the scale of size
are all centered around the female figure. The hideous,
gigantic corporeality of the Brobdingnagian women is represented first in the anti-madonna scene that Gulliver witnesses almost upon his arrival in Brobdingnag—the woman
nursing her child:

> The nurse to quiet her babe made use of a rattle . . . but all in
> vain, so that she was forced to apply the last remedy by giving
> it suck. I must confess no object ever disgusted me so much as
> the sight of her monstrous breast, which I cannot tell what to
> compare with, so as to give the curious reader an idea of its
> bulk, shape and colour. It stood prominent six foot, and
> could not be less than sixteen in circumference. The nipple
> was about half the bigness of my head, and the hue both of
> that and the dug so varified with spots, pimples and freckles,
> that nothing could appear more nauseous . . . . This made me
> reflect upon the fair skins of our English ladies, who appear
> so beautiful to us, only because they are of our own size, and
> their defects not to be seen but through a magnifying glass.[8]

---

8. Jonathan Swift, *Gulliver's Travels*, in *Gulliver's Travels and Other Writ-*

The nauseous scent against which Strephon ought to stop his nose almost overwhelms Gulliver in the apartments of the maids of honour: "They would often strip me naked from top to toe, and lay me at full length in their bosoms; wherewith I was much disgusted; because, to say the truth, a very offensive smell came from their skins" (95). And disease, like that which wastes Celia in "The Progress of Beauty," gives Gulliver his most horrific fantasy of female corruption in Brobdingnag: "One day the governess ordered our coachman to stop at several shops, where the beggars, watching their opportunity, crowded to the sides of the coach, and gave me the most horrible spectacles that ever an European eye beheld. There was a woman with a cancer in her breast, swelled to a monstrous size, full of holes, in two or three of which I could have easily crept, and covered my whole body" (90). Though Gulliver thinks to stop his nose with rue only at the end of part 4, the nauseous scent, the disease and corruption, and the hideous corporeality that we have seen elsewhere in Swift's texts to be so powerfully and specifically associated with the female figure pervade the second voyage of his *Travels*. But if we look to the fourth voyage, we can see all these qualities again embodied in the Yahoos: their stench, their fleshliness, their corruption, and their uncontrolled sexuality are, as we have seen, the attributes essential to the female figure. From this perspective, the whole context of part 4 takes on a new significance. The Yahoos are the prototypical women of Swift's works.

Predictably, Gulliver's account of female luxury in part 4 reproduces the economic trope of the Irish tracts and of Mandeville's more fully-faceted account of the female basis

---

ings, ed. Louis A. Landa (Boston: Houghton Mifflin, 1960), 74. Subsequent references to *Gulliver's Travels* will be to this edition.

of capitalist prosperity: "I assured him, that this whole globe of earth must be at least three times gone round, before one of our better female yahoos could get her breakfast, or a cup to put it in" (203). But Gulliver's relationship with the Yahoos themselves suggests another dimension to the role of the woman in the *Travels*. Gulliver begins at a seemingly unbridgeable distance from the Yahoos, which are represented as some species of monkey, perhaps, having little in common with the human. But the main import of part 4 is the increasing proximity and eventual identification between the Yahoo and the human, despite Gulliver's own resistance and disgust. This process of association with the creatures that seem at first utterly and hideously other suggests a dynamic of aversion and identification that we will find to be central to the ideological significance of the satire. In part 2, likewise, Gulliver's disgust with the maids of honor is balanced by a titillating voyeurism that singles out the "handsomest" and suggests that he is sexually implicated in the scene: figuratively, in the sense that he is evidently desirous himself, but also—and more grotesquely—physically, in that once we entertain the fantasy of a sexual connection between Gulliver and the maids of honor, we are implicitly invited to imagine the actual physical incorporation of the tiny male figure into the body of the woman: "The handsomest among these maids of honour, a pleasant frolicsome girl of sixteen, would sometimes set me astride upon one of her nipples, with many other tricks, wherein the reader will excuse me for not being over particular" (96). The story of the cancerous breast, in this context, supplies a parallel image of explicit incorporation, in which Gulliver responds to the sight of female corruption with the extraordinary and unexpected fantasy of creeping inside and covering his whole body in the "nauseous unwholesome living Carcase" of the diseased woman.

In fact, Gulliver actually does take the place of the female figure at more than one prominent point in the *Travels*. In the relativist comparison between Gulliver's own form as a giant in Lilliput and his encounter with the giants of Brobdingnag, he repeatedly occupies the position of a woman. The overpowering scent of the Brobdingnagian maids of honor puts Gulliver in mind of the occasion in Lilliput when "an intimate friend of mine . . . took the freedom, in a warm day, when I had used a good deal of exercise, to complain of a strong smell about me . . . I suppose his faculty of smelling was as nice with regard to me, as mine was to that of this people" (95). And similarly, in the anti-madonna scene, after describing the "spots, pimples and freckles" of the nursing woman's skin, Gulliver provides a Lilliputian account of his own skin for comparison:

> an intimate friend of mine . . . said that my face appeared much fairer and smoother when he looked on me from the ground, than it did upon a nearer view when I took him up in my hand, and brought him close, which he confessed was at first a very shocking sight. He said he could discover great holes in my skin . . . and my complexion made up of several colours altogether disagreeable . . . On the other side discoursing of the ladies in that emperor's court, he used to tell me, one had freckles, another too wide a mouth, a third too large a nose, nothing of which I was able to distinguish. (74–75)

These comparisons too establish a routine and consistent interchangeability between Gulliver and the female figures of his narrative.

Similarly, in part 2 Gulliver is dressed by his little nurse, Glumdalclitch, in a manner that would have evoked a common contemporary female image. As Neil McKendrick has shown, the fashion doll was the major implement of the rise and popularization of female fashion in the eighteenth century. Descended from life-sized dolls imported from France and displayed in the London shops wearing the latest Parisian dresses, the miniature fashion doll was widely available in rural as well as urban parts of England. Supplied with sample suits of the latest designs, they were dressed both by clothing merchants and by children and adult women, and served as a major means of teaching the new and unfamiliar concept of rapidly changing styles, and of spreading the notion of a market-conditioned obsolescence.[9] In Brobdingnag, Gulliver plays precisely this role; for Glumdalclitch and the contemporary reader he takes the place of this miniaturized, commodified female figure.

To say that Gulliver occupies the place of the woman at recurrent moments is not to say that Gulliver is the same as a woman, but to suggest a systematic pattern of implication, which moves from the various forms of interchangeability that we have seen in Gulliver's connection with the fashion doll and the Yahoos to a full incorporation like that offered by Gulliver's relation to the cancerous breast and the maids of honor, and which begins to problematize Swift's attack on women and to complicate our understanding of his relation with the female other. Gulliver's implicit identification with the female figure—a figure we have discovered to be systematically underlying the ideology of mercantile capitalism—suggests that *Gulliver's Travels* must be read in the context of that major historical conjuncture. Those panegyrics on women that I cited earlier to exemplify the mercantile capitalist context of Swift's misogyny unconsciously function, as we saw, to displace responsibility for the historical consequences of capitalism upon womankind, to make

9. Neil McKendrick, "The Commercialization of Fashion," in Neil McKendrick, John Brewer, and J. H. Plumb, *The Birth of a Consumer Society: The Commercialization of Eighteenth-Century England* (Bloomington: Indiama University Press, 1982), 43–49.

her a locus for the male anxieties of empire. Swift's Irish tracts certainly participate in this common assumption of displaced responsibility, though with a different valuation. But the implicit dynamic of aversion and identification that we have begun to discern in *Gulliver's Travels* suggests that in this major text that effort of displacement partly fails, that the shifting status of the male observer (which we have been taught by formalist criticism of Swift to describe as the "persona controversy") makes the designation of a separable other, upon whom the anxieties and responsibilities of mercantile capitalism and imperialism can be displaced, symptomatically impossible.

But symptomatic of what? Here in order to invoke the dialectical connection of gender and race toward which I have been aiming, we must turn to another fictional account, contemporary with *Gulliver's Travels*, at least as disturbing, and much more offensive. This is the account that we can construct from the writings of travelers, naturalists, and colonialists of the nature and society of the Negro in what they describe as his native habitat in Africa or under slavery in the colonies of the new world. Unlike *Gulliver's Travels*, of course, this fiction was accepted as objective testimony in the travel literature and ultimately encoded as science in the most widely read volumes of travel and natural history through the middle of the next century.[10] At stake was the proximity of the Negro to man or ape on the chain of being. And those two standards of deviation determined the definition of the Negro race. Janet Schaw, in her journal of a voyage to the West Indies and North Carolina (1774), spontaneously reproduces, in her account of her

10. See Sander Gilman, "Black Bodies, White Bodies: Toward an Iconography of Female Sexuality in Late Nineteenth-Century Art, Medicine, and Literature," in *Critical Inquiry* 12 (1985): 204–42.

first sight of Negro children upon her arrival in Antigua, an association quite typical of the period: "Just as we got into the lane, a number of pigs run out at a door, and after them a parcel of monkeys. This not a little surprized me, but I found what I took for monkeys were negro children, naked as they were born."[11] Schaw's "natural" mistake suggests the popular and commonplace status of this symptomatic European racist confusion.

If we juxtapose the details of two prominent contemporary accounts which served as compendia of seventeenth and eighteenth-century observations of the inhabitants of Africa, we can set the context for Janet Schaw's observation. George Louis Leclerc Buffon's massive and influential *Natural History* (relevant volumes in French, 1749–60) and Edward Long's *History of Jamaica* (1774) both summarize accounts of the Negro from earlier writings in French and English dating from the early seventeenth century on.[12]

11. Janet Schaw, *Journal of a Lady of Quality . . .* , ed. Evangeline Walker Andrews and Charles McLean Andrews (New Haven: Yale University Press, 1922), 78.

12. Among the relevant additional sources are Wouter Schouten, *Voyages de Gautier Schouten aux Indes orientales, commence l'an 1658 & fini l'an 1665* (trans. from the Dutch), 2 vols. (Paris, 1725); Claude Counte de Forbin *Memoires du Compte de Forbin* (Paris, 1729); Pierre Francoise Xavier de Charlevoix, *Histoire de L'isle Espagnole ou de S. Domingue* (Paris, 1730–31), *History of Paraguay* (Paris, 1757; London, 1769), and *Histoire de la Nouvelle France* (Paris, 1744); Jean Baptiste Dutertre, *Histoire Generale des Antilles* (Paris, 1654); Willem Bosman, *New and Accurate Description of the Coast of Guinea* (trans. from the Dutch) (London, 1705; reprint, 1721); Sir Hans Sloane, *A Voyage To the Islands Madera, Barbados, Nieves, S. Christophers and Jamaica . . .* (London, 1707). Furthermore, A. H. Mackinnon describes the Augustans' fascination with the native "other" as depicted particularly in the narratives of William Dampier, *A New Voyage Round the World* (London, 1697); François Leguat, *A New Voyage to the East Indies* (1708); and Woodes Rogers, *A Cruizing Voyage Round the World* (London, 1712); he suggests that Swift may have been influenced by Dampier and Woodes Rogers. See "The Augustan Intellectual and the Ignoble Savage: Houyhnhym versus Hottentot," in *Essays on English and American Literature*

Buffon and Long actually take opposite positions on Negroes, Buffon arguing, against contemporary sentiment, that they are of the same species as Europeans, and Long arguing, against Buffon, that "they are a different species of the same *genus*": "Let us not then doubt, but that every member of the creation is wisely fitted and adapted to the certain uses, and confined within the certain bounds, to which it was ordained by the Divine Fabricator. The measure of the several orders and varieties of these Blacks may be as compleat as that of any other race of mortals; filling up that space, or degree, beyond which they are not destined to pass; and discriminating them from the rest of men, not in *kind*, but in *species*."[13]

But though they arrive at very different conclusions, Long and Buffon produce very similar accounts. Buffon sets up the comparison between apes and Negroes most explicitly:

> To form a proper judgment between them, a savage man and an ape should be viewed together; for we have no just idea of man in a pure state of nature. The head covered with bristly hairs, or with curled wool; the face partly hid by a long beard, and still longer hairs in the front, which surround his eyes, and make them appear sunk in his head, like those of the brutes; the lips thick and projecting, the nose flat, the aspect wild or stupid; the ears, body, and limbs are covered with hair, the nails long, thick, and crooked . . . the breasts of the female long and flabby, and the skin of her belly hanging down to her knees; the children wallowing in filth, and crawling on their hands and feet; and, in short, the adults sitting on their hams, forming an hideous appearance, rendered more so by being besmeared all over with stinking grease.

---

and a Sheaf of Poems, ed. J. Bakker and J. A. Verleun (Amsterdam: Rodopi, 1987).

13. Edward Long, *The History of Jamaica . . .* , 3 vols. (London, 1774), 1:356 and 375. Subsequent references will be to this edition.

This sketch, drawn from a savage Hottentot [a Negro], is still a flattering portrait, for there is as great a distance between a man in a pure state of nature and a Hottentot, as there is between a Hottentot and us. But if we wish to compare the human species with that of the ape, we must add to it the affinities of organization, the agreements of temperament, the vehement desire of the males for the females, the like conformation of the genitals in both sexes, the periodic emanations of the females, the compulsive or voluntary intermixture of the negresses with the apes, the produce of which has united into both species; and then consider, supposing them not of the same species, how difficult it is to discover the interval by which they are separated.[14]

Buffon, unlike Long, ultimately dismisses the argument that apes and Negroes are of the same species; in other words, this passage indicates the position of a defender of the Negro's humanity.

The themes of nakedness, filth, and stench persist in this and in Long's account, alongside claims for nimbleness in climbing, running, or swimming (*History of Jamaica* 365). Long describes as one of the Negro's distinctive features "their bestial or fetid smell" (352). Buffon argues that the Hottentots are not true Negroes, but rather whites who make themselves dirty by wallowing in filth, noting that "they seldom live longer than 40 years; and this short duration of life is doubtless caused by their being continually covered with filth, and living chiefly upon meat that is cor-

14. George Louis Leclerc Buffon, *Buffon's Natural History. Containing a Theory of the Earth, A General History of Man, of the Brute Creation, and of Vegatables, Minerals, etc.*, 10 vols. (London, 1797), 9:136–37. Subsequent references will be to this edition. A recent note describing a contemporary influence upon Swift's depiction of the Yahoo suggests another sort of connection between Yahoo and Hottentot: in terms of the debate over the "natural man." This Hottentot, however, represents a philosophical rather than a racial category. See Daniel Eilon, "Swift's Yahoo and Leslie's Hottentot," *Notes and Queries* n.s. 30 (1983): 510–12.

rupted" (*Buffon's Natural History* 298–99). Numerous reports summarized by these writers describe the Negro's habit of eating carrion: in Long's words, "They are most brutal in their manners and uncleanly in their diet, eating flesh almost raw by choice, though intolerably putrid and full of maggots" (*History of Jamaica* 382); "at their meals they tear the meat with their talons, and chuck it by handfulls down their throats with all the voracity of wild beasts" (383).

Buffon's and Long's accounts agree that Negroes are incapable of civil government. According to Long: "In general, they are void of genius, and seem almost incapable of making any progress in civility or science. They have no plan or system of morality among them. . . . They have no moral sensations" (353). "In regard to their laws and government, these may, with them, be more properly ranged under the title of customs and manners; they have no regulations dictated by foresight . . . they seem to have no polity, nor any comprehension of the use of civil institutions" (378). "Their genius (if it can be so called) consists alone in trick and cunning, enabling them, like monkeys and apes, to be thievish and mischievous, with a peculiar dexterity. They seem unable to combine ideas, or pursue a chain of reasoning" (377). In short, they are "a brutish, ignorant, idle, crafty, treacherous, bloody, thievish, mistrustful, and superstitious people" (354).

Buffon summarizes various visitors' explanations for the difference between the facial features of Negroes and those of white Europeans; blacks have flat noses and faces from being carried against their mother's chests:

> While at work or travelling, the Negro-women almost always carry their infants on their backs. To this custom some travellers ascribe the flat nose and big bellies among Negroes; since the woman, from necessarily giving sudden jerks, is apt

to strike the nose of the child against her back; who in order
to avoid the blow, keeps its head back by pushing its belly
forward. . . . Father du Tertre says expressly, that if most
negroes are flat-nosed, it is because the parents crush the
noses of their children . . . and that those who escape these
operations, their features are as comely as those of the Europeans. (*Buffon's Natural History* 282–83)

One need not be a close reader of part 4 of *Gulliver's
Travels* to pick up the numerous echoes there of this other
major eighteenth-century fantasy of difference: Swift's Yahoos are "prodigiously nimble from their infancy" (214);
their countenances, too, are "flat and broad, the nose de-
pressed, the lips large, and the mouth wide. . . distorted by
. . . suffering their infants to lie grovelling on the earth, or
by carrying them on their backs, nuzzling with their face
against the mother's shoulders" (186). The picture that
Gulliver provides upon his first glimpse of the Yahoos
sounds very much like Buffon's image of the natural man
or the Hottentot:

Their heads and breasts were covered with a thick hair, some
frizzled and others lank; they had beards like goats . . . they
climbed high trees, as nimbly as a squirrel, for they had
strong extended claws before and behind, terminating in
sharp points, and hooked. They would often spring, and
bound, and leap with prodigious agility. The females were
not so large as the males; they had long lank hair on their
heads, and only a sort of down on the rest of their bodies. . . .
Their dugs hung between their fore-feet, and often reached
almost to the ground as they walked. . . . Upon the whole, I
never beheld in all my travels so disagreeable an animal, or
one against which I naturally conceived so strong antipathy.
(181)

Gulliver makes much of their nakedness, distinguishing
himself from the Yahoos by emphasizing his own clothes.

Their bodily hair, their "strange disposition to nasti-
ness and dirt" (212), their stench—especially the "offensive
smell" of the female Yahoos (213)—all belong to the eighteenth-century accounts of racial difference focusing on the
Negro. Furthermore, the Yahoos feed mainly upon raw
flesh:

> I saw three of those detestable creatures . . . feeding upon . . .
> the flesh of some animals, which I afterwards found to be
> that of asses and dogs, and now and then a cow dead by acci-
> dent or disease. . . . they held their food between the claws of
> their forefeet, and tore it with their teeth. . . . [The Houy-
> hnhnm] brought out of the yahoo's kennel a piece of ass's
> flesh, but it smelt so offensively that I turned from it with
> loathing: he then threw it to the yahoo, by whom it was
> greedily devoured. (186)

And they are by definition incapable of reason or government; according to Gulliver "the yahoos appear to be
the most unteachable of all animals, their capacities never
reaching higher than to draw or carry burthens. Yet I am
of opinion this defect ariseth chiefly from a perverse, res-
tive disposition. For they are cunning, malicious, treacherous and revengeful. They are strong and hardy, but of a
cowardly spirit, and by consequence insolent, abject, and
cruel" (214–15).

But perhaps one of the most commonplace anecdotes of
eighteenth-century racial fantasy was that of the sexual
connection between Negroes and apes or orang-outangs
alluded to in those arguments about the species of the Negro. These stories represent a kind of radical miscegenation that evidently captured the imagination of Swift's contemporaries. We can encounter several versions of the story
retold by both Buffon and Long. Long's conclusions summarize his notion that whites and Negroes are different

species, since the import of this story is that Negroes and apes are the same:

> It is also averred, that [orang-outangs] sometimes endeavour to surprize and carry off Negroe women into their woody retreats, in order to enjoy them . . . that they conceive a Passion for the Negroe women, and hence must be supposed to covet their embraces from a natural impulse of desire, such as inclines one animal towards another of the same species, or which has a conformity in the organs of generation . . . [which may be taken as proof that] the oran-outang and some races of black men are very nearly allied. (360, 364, 370)

At this point, we need hardly remind ourselves of the encounter that teaches Gulliver that he is "a real yahoo in every limb and feature":

> [As he is bathing in a stream], a young female yahoo, standing behind a bank . . . and inflamed by desire . . . came running with all speed, and leaped into the water within five yards of the place where I bathed. I was never in my life so terribly frighted. . . . She embraced me after a most fulsome manner; I roared as loud as I could and the nag [his protector] came galloping towards me, whereupon she quitted her grasp, with the utmost reluctancy, and leaped upon the opposite bank, where she stood gazing and howling all the time I was putting on my clothes. . . . now I could no longer deny that I was a real yahoo . . . since the females had a natural propensity to me as one of their own species. (215)

The Yahoos' greatest threat to Gulliver is here epitomized in the figure of the female whose sexuality stands as proof of the identification with the other that Gulliver abhors.

In short, part 4 of *Gulliver's Travels* is essentially compiled from contemporary evidence of racial difference derived from accounts of the race that was in this period most immediately and visibly the object and human implement of mercantile capitalist expansion. I do not mean by this that the Yahoos are meant to stand for African blacks in any straightforward allegorical fashion. Indeed, the Houyhnhnms also participate in this general allusion to the cultural experience of imperialism: for example, their aversion to untruth is modeled upon the common contemporary notion that native peoples cannot lie.[15] What we have observed in part 4 of *Gulliver's Travels* is not an allegory, but a pervasive contextualization in which the shifting status of the male observer, the dynamic of aversion and implication, difference and incorporation, that we have already observed in Swift's satire is given a specific historical referent: the institutionalization of racism in the service of empire.

Swift's miscegenation scene—in which the female Yahoo sets upon the male European—gives us an opportunity to define the mutual interaction of gender and race that shapes this text's relation to history. In this period, and even into the nineteenth century, accounts of the sexual attraction between apes and Negroes were invariably represented as exchanges between a male ape or orang-outang and a Negro woman.[16] The anecdote in Swift's text, in which the human male is set upon by an apparently bestial female, stands out for its evident violation of the sexual categories of this racist fantasy. Why, at this point, should Swift's text tamper with the materials that constitute the satire's representation of difference? The reversal of sexual roles in this scene could be seen as part of the persistent

15. For instance, of the Mosquitos Indians, "there is nothing more hateful to them than breach of Promise, or telling an Untruth, their Words being inviolable" (Sloane, *A Voyage To the Islands Madera, Barbados, Nieves, S. Christophers and Jamaica . . .* , 1:lxxvii).

16. See Sander Gilman's "Black Bodies, White Bodies," for a description of the focus on the sexuality of the female Negro, with the corollary absence of any interest at all in the sexuality of the male.

dynamic of identification or interchangeability that we found in Gulliver's relation to the female figure elsewhere. Once again Gulliver is taking the place that the woman would occupy in the contemporary imagination. Or is he? Isn't it equally relevant to read this reversal as a racial interchangeability, in which the white European Gulliver takes the place of the Negro, the Yahoo takes the place of the ape, and the question of species is ironically restated? To see Gulliver as the Negro here, when the Yahoo has so consistently taken that role, is a striking new version of interchangeability that figures a significant reversal of the construction of racial difference. Programmatically, if in contemporary racist ideology the ape's lust for the Negro is supposed to prove them to be of the same (nonhuman) species, then by the logic of Swift's satire the Yahoo's lust for Gulliver, the Negro's for the white European, proves them to be of the same species as well, equally human or nonhuman. By placing Gulliver in the position of the woman, this scene has simultaneously placed him in the position of the Negro.

Like the female other in relation to the male observer in parts 1 and 2 of *Gulliver's Travels* and in the misogynist poetry, the native other of part 4 stands in a contradictory relationship with the colonialist, a relationship of aversion and implication, difference and incorporation. And Gulliver's position in this voyage—simultaneously identified with and absolutely differentiated from the Yahoo—itself suggests the contradictory nature of identity in Swift's redaction of the colonialist fantasy. The colonialist, for that reason, cannot reconcile himself to his own reflection in the mirror: "When I happened to behold the reflection of my own form in a lake or fountain, I turned away my face in horror and detestation of myself, and could better endure the sight of a common yahoo, than of my own person" (225). The dynamic of difference and incorporation that

characterizes this text makes it inevitable that Gulliver's ultimate efforts "to behold my figure often in a glass, and
thus if possible habituate myself by time to tolerate the
sight of a human creature" (238) must by definition be futile. On the one hand, the fourth voyage brings Gulliver
into contact with an absolutely alien and hideous other, in
the face of which all the brutality of colonialist repression,
genocide included, must seem justified. On the other hand,
it proposes an intense identification with and incorporation
by the native that destabilizes any secure constitution of a
distinct colonialist subject and even suggests an implicit critique of such a position.

The mutual interaction of the native and the woman
through the mediation of the fictional Gulliver reproduces
the historical relationship between imperialist exploitation
abroad, with its economic dependence on slavery, and commodification at home, with its ideological emphasis on the
figure of the woman. Thus Swift's satire registers the complex interdependency of categories of the oppressed in this
period of English imperialism, and the interchangeability
figured in part 4 enables us to move beyond misogyny in
itself or racism in itself to a dialectical critique that provides
equal priority to both gender and race. Neither Swift's contemporaries nor Swift himself would have been able to
move, as I have done here, from the misogynist attack on
women to an understanding of its historical basis in commodification and trade. On the other hand, the active undermining of the ideology of racial superiority that we have
observed in *Gulliver's Travels* certainly would have been accessible to an eighteenth-century audience. Contemporary
readers—steeped in the racist images associated with English colonialism in that period and indeed through the
mid-nineteenth century—would have been much more
ready than modern ones to register the crucial evocations
of racial difference in part 4, and much quicker than we

are to pick up that text's pervasive playing with ideas of racial superiority and its perverse leveling of whites and nonwhites to one common depravity. Indeed, the vitality and cultural power of *Gulliver's Travels*, and perhaps even its longevity in the canon of English literature, may be explained in part by the fact that it represented a challenge to an ideology that itself had a vital and powerful current function.

Let me return to the programmatic and polemical mode with which I began this chapter, and with which I introduced the premises of this book. This reading of Swift exemplifies my claims to a radical political criticism and to a particular kind of critical truth. I want here to bring that truth into a final focus. Let's say that this account shows that Swift's misogyny is appropriately understood in the context of mercantile capitalism, that the structure of that misogyny opens up a critique of the treatment of racial difference essential to Swift's strategy in a crucial part of *Gulliver's Travels* and accessible from the moment of its publication. Why should we see these conclusions, and not other arguments that might be equally subtle in their use of historical context, as radical? This argument describes a certain odd configuration within a dominant ideology, certain surprising articulations among misogyny, imperialism, and racism. It should be no surprise to find that eighteenth-century imperialism is both misogynist and racist. The political utility might arise first through seeing that these two forms of oppression—misogyny and racism—are not independent variables within a hegemonic edifice, but interdependent categories with mutualities of their own. But this reading of Swift also suggests that a basis for opposition can arise out of the interdependence of different forms of oppression: the unpromising materials of misogyny enable us to perceive the critique of racism. The sacrifice of women might seem a high price to pay for the problematiz-ation of racial difference. Ironically, though, it is this price that distinguishes a literary criticism of a distinctly libera-tionist cast from one more generally committed to a politi-cized thematic. The extreme case of Swift that I have been pursuing here is the rule rather than the exception; its ulti-mate political utility as I see it is as a positive model and not as a negative lesson. The lesson it might teach some critics is to infer from the compromised or problematic historical situation in which we always find ourselves the appropriate-ness of defeatism or despair. This lesson authorizes a criti-cism of withdrawal. But the model it provides is one of ar-ticulation and interdependence—the difficult negotiations that are the point of departure of a liberationist politics.

Let's say that Swift's travesty of true consciousness is the true radical political criticism. And let's say that the end of empire is only truly possible when we see the extent to which we have been serving the ends of empire.

Index

Fashion doll, 186–87
Female Soldier (Hannah Snell),
    142–43
Fielding, Henry, 8; *Champion*,
    111–12; *Juvenalis Satyra Sexta*,
    140–41; *Tom Jones*, 141
Fox, George, 54
Francis, Lord Willoughby, 52,
    55

Gildon, Charles, 110, 126
Goreau, Angeline, 24
Greenblatt, Stephen, 31
Greene, Edward Burnaby, 140–
    41

Harley, Robert, 45, 52, 55
Hawkesworth, John, 25
Hervey, John (Lord Fanny), 1,
    124
Hill, Aaron, 66; *Fatal Extrava-
    gance*, 88
Hill, Christopher, 90

JanMohamed, Abdul, 29–30,
    32, 36–37
Jehlen, Myra, 48
Johnson, Charles, 66
Johnson, Samuel, 143–44
Juvenal, 138–41, 145, 154–55,
    175

Kenner, Hugh, 109–10

LaFayette, Madame de, 39
Lee, Nathaniel, 38, 65; *Rival
    Queens*, 67
Lillo, George, 66; *Fatal Curiosity*,
    86, 88; *London Merchant*, 68,
    86–88, 99
Long, Edward, 189–92, 194–95

McKendrick, Neil, 90, 112, 186–
    87
McKeon, Michael, 8
Mandeville, Bernard, 112, 114–
    16, 175, 178, 180, 184–85
Marx, Karl, 34, 119–20, 132–33
Misogyny, 16, 20, 22, 73, 74,
    99–101, 114, 123, 156–57,
    170–200

Moore, Edward, 66; *Gamester*, 88

Novak, Maximillian, 8

Orrery, Roger Boyle, Earl of, 38
Otway, Thomas, 15, 65; *Orphan*,
    67–74, 77, 79, 82; *Venice Pre-
    served*, 67, 74
Owen, Edward, 141

Pope, Alexander, 2, 3, 7, 44, 97,
    103–34, 148, 175, 177; *Epistle
    to a Lady*, 123, 125–26, 128;
    Epistle to Burlington, 132; *Essay
    on Criticism*, 108–9, 126–29,
    132; *Rape of the Lock*, 108,
    113–14, 144–46, 149, 154,
    156; *Sober Advice from Horace*,
    (*Second Satire of the First Book
    of Horace*), 121–26, 128–31,
    134; *Windsor Forest*, 118
Pratt, Mary Louise, 39
Purchas, Samuel, 158, 159

Quakers, 54

Race, 13–14, 17, 23–63, 135–
    69, 170–200
Raleigh, Walter, 158, 160, 161
Richardson, Jonathan (father
    and son), 111
Richardson, Samuel, 7, 97–98
Richetti, John, 8
Rochester, John Wilmot, Earl
    of, 25, 175
Rowe, Nicholas, 44, 65, 66, 77;
    Ambitious Step-Mother, 68, 76;
    Fair Penitent, 77, 80; *Jane
    Shore*, 15, 77, 80–86, 101,
    117, 133, 149, 177, 180; *Lady
    Jane Gray*, 77
Royal African Company, 163

Said, Edward, 29, 30, 32–33
Sandford, Robert, 52
Sartre, Jean-Paul, 27
Schaw, Janet, 188–89
Scot, William, 53
Scudery, Madeleine de, 39

Library of Congress Cataloging-in-Publication Data

Brown, Laura, 1949–
    Ends of empire : women and ideology in early eighteenth-century
English literature / Laura Brown.
        p.   cm.
    Includes bibliographical references and index.
    ISBN 0-8014-2850-5. — ISBN 0-8014-8095-7 (pbk.)
        1. English literature—18th century—History and criticism.
    2. Literature and society—Great Britain—History—18th century.
    3. Women and literature—Great Britain—History—18th century.
    4. Social problems in literature.   5. Race relations in literature.
    6. Imperialism in literature.   7. Sex role in literature.
    I. Title.
    PR448.S64B76   1993
    820.9'005—dc20   92-36853